Complete Book of
Teddy Bears

Joan Greene
Ted Menten

PUBLICATIONS INTERNATIONAL, LTD.

ISBN 0-88176-561-9

Library of Congress Catalog Card Number:
88-63580

Joan Greene (Venturino) owns Bears To Go at Ghiradelli Square, San Francisco, one of the oldest all-teddy-bear stores in the United States. She published the first catalog for handmade teddy bears and is responsible for focusing national attention on teddy bears as an art form. Joan also writes stories about teddy bears and the people who love them.

Ted Menten is an accomplished designer, photographer, collector, bearmaker, and writer. His many books on teddy bears include *The Teddy Bear Lovers Catalog, The World According to HUG,* and *Teddy's Bearzaar.* His articles on collectibles appeared regularly in *Dolls* magazine. Ted is now the editorial and creative force behind *Teddy Bear Review,* a quarterly magazine entirely devoted to teddy bears.

Table of Contents

Table of Contents

Introduction

When you imagine the perfect teddy bear, you may remember the friend and companion of your childhood whose fur was worn thin by hugs, or you may think of a pristine Steiff bear, a teddy dressed as your favorite nursery-rhyme character, or even cuddly Snuggle bouncing across your TV screen. Teddy bears are so much a part of childhood in America that few of us can imagine growing up without a bear, and not many grown-ups can resist the appealing glint in a teddy bear's eye and love-me smile on a teddy's furry little face.

Teddy bears trace their lineage back to 1902 and a bear that President Teddy Roosevelt did not shoot. Teddy bears have come a long way since a political cartoon satirizing the president's bear hunt inspired the first American teddy-bear makers to begin making stuffed bears and encouraged the importing of German-made teddy bears. This book chronicles the history and evolution of teddy bears from their enormous popularity during first decade of this century until today's renaissance of affection for teddies. While the great old teddy bears were produced mostly by large toymakers, today's best teddies are made by individual bearmakers as well as toy companies. In the following pages, you'll meet some of the most-accomplished teddy-bear makers and learn about the companies that manufacture the most-endearing teddy bears. Best of all you'll find hundreds of beautiful full-color photographs of the cutest and most-lovable teddy bears you've ever seen. Some are dressed in their fanciful best; others need no further adornment than a ribbon bow, but all these teddy bears look you right in the eye and say, in the silent way that teddy bears tell us what is in their hearts, "Love me; I'll always be your friend."

The History & Evolution of Teddy Bears

The identity of the very first teddy bear is a subject of much dispute. Some people say he was German; others are sure that he was English. In the United States, most people believe that the forebear of all teddy bears was American. There are many more legends about the origin of the teddy bear than there are facts. But if a particular account of the early days of teddy bears cannot be proved, it hardly matters. When it comes to teddy bears, we're going to believe what we want to believe.

The basic story of the original teddy bear goes like this: On a hunting trip in Mississippi in 1902, the president of the United States, Theodore Roosevelt, did *not* shoot a bear. Clifford Berryman, a well-known illustrator and political cartoonist, felt that this was a newsworthy event and drew a cartoon for the *Washington Post.* Two toymakers, one in Germany and the other in New York, also play significant roles in the legend. At the same time that the president was off hunting in Mississippi, Margarete Steiff was in her workroom in Germany creating delightful stuffed animals. Rose Michtom and her husband were hard at work in their confectioner's shop in New York, unaware that a political cartoon was about to change their lives.

Ideal teddy bear made in the early 1900s.

Forebears

The President's Bear Hunt

President Roosevelt's hunting trip was big news; it was the first time he had gotten completely away from his official duties since he entered the White House. All the newspapers carried stories about it, including the *New York Times,* the *Washington Evening Star,* and the *Washington Post.* The press reports followed the president from Cincinnati through Kentucky to his destination in Smedes, Mississippi, which is about 25 miles north of Vicksburg. The president planned to spend four days hunting and relaxing. President Roosevelt was an experienced bear hunter; he had hunted grizzlies in the Rockies. But in Mississippi he planned to hunt bear on horseback with hounds, and this was a new experience for him.

The president's party reached their hunting camp on November 13, 1902. The party included several prominent businessmen, John M. Parker of New Orleans, and the well-known bear hunter, H. L. Foote, who was considered to be one of the best shooters in Mississippi. Holt Collier, a former scout for the Confederate Army, was in charge of the hounds. The campsite was located 15 miles east of Smedes on the banks of the Little Sunflower River. The area was virtually unbroken wilderness; no one lived within miles of the camp. The forest was made up primarily of ash, oak, and cypress trees, and was choked with thick underbrush. A trail had to be cut to reach the campsite. Horses were provided for the hunting party.

The morning of November 14 was clear and cold. President Roosevelt, who slept the night in a tent, was photographed dressed in his hunting clothes (riding trousers, heavy leather leggings, a flannel shirt, a corduroy coat, and a brown slouch hat). President Roosevelt sat astride his horse and waited for the dogs to catch the scent of bear. When they got the scent, the president and his guides plunged through the dense undergrowth in pursuit. Within minutes the dogs had located the bear. Holt Collier knew from his years of experience

Teddy bears campaign for Roosevelt, from left to right: an early humped-back bear (9 inches tall), a handmade 6½-inch teddy, and a 13-inch bear, made in the 1930s and dressed like T.R. in a wool coat, felt hat, and glasses.

where the bear was likely to make an appearance. Collier directed the president along a trail to a likely cut-off point, and Mr. Foote and the president rode off.

The forest was thick, making riding difficult. From time to time, swamp deer darted across the trail, but neither the president nor Mr. Foote took a shot at them. They were on a bear hunt, and they were primarily interested in finding the bear that the dogs were chasing. By noon they realized that the bear must have turned and gone off in another direction. The sound of the barking dogs grew more distant. Mr. Foote and the president returned to camp for lunch.

According to the newspaper accounts of the hunt, if Mr. Foote and the president had stayed where they were instead of returning to camp for lunch, President Roosevelt would very likely have had the opportunity to shoot at and possibly kill a bear. With the pack of yapping dogs at his heels, the bear turned again and headed back in the direction he had started. He must have crossed at almost the exact spot where Holt Collier had positioned the president. If President Roosevelt had shot the bear, there might be no teddy bears today.

While most of the hunting party pursued the bear, the president enjoyed his lunch at the base camp. The bear was eventually exhausted by running from the dogs and ran into a water hole where he took a stance against them. Standing on his hind legs, the bear took one sweep after another at the hounds, knocking the barking dogs aside. Holt Collier rode up, and when he saw what was going on, jumped from his horse and knocked the bear over with a blow from his rifle butt. Collier roped the still-dazed bear and tied him to a tree. He sounded his horn to proclaim that the bear had been brought to bay and then sent a messenger to go get the president.

When President Roosevelt arrived on the scene, he refused to shoot the bear and would not permit anyone else to shoot it. He instructed Mr. Parker to put the animal out of its misery, and John Parker killed the bear with his hunting knife. The president was a true sportsman; he refused to shoot a defenseless bear. Even though over time teddy bears have come to represent a great deal more than good sportsmanship, this moment when the president insisted on doing the right thing marks the beginning of the legend of the teddy bear.

While the president's bear hunt may seem cruel by today's standards, it must be viewed from a historical perspective. Theodore Roosevelt loved animals and was a sincere protector of the environment. In 1902 few animals were perceived to be in immediate danger of extinction. While today we feel that many animals need our protection, at that time hunting was a much more generally acceptable sport. By refusing to shoot the helpless bear, the president was demonstrating

the concern and tenderheartedness for which he is remembered and which teddy bears have come to represent.

The Berryman Cartoon

While the president was hunting bear, Clifford Berryman, a popular political cartoonist, was looking for a humorous way to comment on the political events of the day. Like all satirists, Berryman exaggerated events for the sake of a chuckle. While many political satirists have hard eyes and sharp tongues, Berryman was relatively gentle with his car-

*The leather muzzle on this early **Steiff** bear is a reminder that even toy bears used to be associated with wild creatures. He is 24 inches tall, jointed, and stuffed with straw.*

toonist's pen and never seemed to set out to hurt anyone's feelings or reputation.

Clifford Berryman knew the president well. Even though he was not on the bear hunt, he was sure that President Roosevelt had acted as the reports indicated. His cartoon of the event as it appeared on November 16, 1902, shows a slim President Roosevelt dressed for hunting and a large bear that's being held on a rope by another man. In a second version of the cartoon that appeared later and is more finished, the president appears heavier and the bear looks more like a cute baby cub. The second version is the more familiar one, and Berryman later began using a similar bear cub in most of his cartoons about the president. Berryman's cartoon refers to both the hunting trip itself and a dispute over state boundaries that was being settled by the president. The cartoon was captioned "Drawing the Line in Mississippi," referring to both of these events.

Berryman drew a second cartoon about the hunt. It appeared in the *Washington Post* on November 19, 1902. In this cartoon a little bear cub is being dragged along by a rope. Dozens of hunters, trackers, woodsmen, photographers, and reporters are following the bear. In the background, there's a large horse-drawn wagon with the words "Canine Ambulance" emblazoned on its side. On top of the wagon is an unconscious hunting dog. The title of this Berryman cartoon is "After a Twentieth Century Bear Hunt."

Clifford Berryman continued to draw bears in cartoons about the president. He changed the bear's shape and character. In the original cartoon the bear was large, mature, and not very appealing. But by the third cartoon the bear had become a cute, wide-eyed bear cub.

Before the end of that year, the delightful cub was a familiar character to the *Washington Post* readers. On December 25, 1902, Berryman drew a cartoon about the little bear himself. It's captioned "Christmas Dreams" and pictures the tiny bruin sitting up in a brass bed in front of the White House. The cub has just awakened from a nightmare featuring a giant bearskin covering one side of the White House.

On Theodore Roosevelt's inauguration day (March 4, 1905), the *Washington Post* featured Berryman's cartoon of "Roosevelt's Bear" on page one. The cartoon is drawn like a comic

Roosevelt the Laughing Teddy Bear was made in 1908. He is 16 inches tall, made of mohair, and stuffed with newspaper.

inda Mullins designed this teddy bear to look like the cub Berryman's cartoons. He's a **Steiff** bear.

This American-made teddy bear probably dates from Theodore Roosevelt's reelection campaign. He is 16 inches tall, made of mohair, and has glass eyes.

teddy bears had become the most-popular toys in American history.

Rose Michtom is believed to have created the first teddy bear. There is very little hard evidence to support this claim, but Rose and her husband, Morris, are certainly the strongest American contenders for the honor. Morris Michtom is believed to have seen Berryman's cartoon reprinted in the *New York Herald.* He suggested that Rose make a toy bear, and she made the first teddy bear. It was about two and a half feet tall and had shoe-button eyes. Michtom wrote to the president to ask for permission to call his wife's bears "Teddy's Bears." The president is supposed to have responded that as far as he was concerned Michtom could use his name, but he doubted that his nickname was of any value. These letters have never been found, so there's no record of anyone ever asking the president's permission to use his name.

The first teddy bears were sold in the Michtoms' confectionery, but soon Rose and Morris Michtom closed their shop and opened a new business, the Ideal Novelty and Toy Company. (The name was later shortened to the Ideal Toy Company.) This family-owned company created many of the finest American-made toys, including teddy bears and Shirley Temple dolls. One of the original Ideal teddy bears now lives in the Smithsonian Institution in Washington, D.C.

Margarete Steiff

This American tale about the advent of teddy bears has an important German element—a charming toymaker named Margarete Steiff. As a child Margarete was stricken with polio. Undaunted by her paralysis, she studied

strip in a series of eight boxes. Each box is captioned with a date to tell the story of the evolution of the bear. Berryman always referred to the tiny cub as "Roosevelt's bear," while the president reportedly called the cub "Berryman's bear."

The First Teddy Bear

During Theodore Roosevelt's term of office, the tiny bear often appeared in Berryman's cartoons. By 1909, the year in which William H. Taft succeeded Roosevelt as president,

These well-loved teddy bears were probably made by the **Ideal Toy Company.** *They were manufactured before 1920.*

*This 16-inch mohair **Steiff** bear has an elephant button in its ear and was manufactured around 1903.*

dressmaking and was the first person in her town, Giengen, to own a sewing machine. While she was still a young girl, Margarete opened her first business, a dress shop for ladies and their children.

In 1880 Margarete created tiny elephant pincushions as gifts for her nieces and nephews. When Margarete transformed a pincushion into a toy elephant, she set a course that eventually would lead her to found one of the greatest toy companies in the world.

In 1897 Margarete's nephew Richard joined her company. While Margarete is usually considered to be the premier German bearmaker, Richard may actually have made the first Steiff bear. He had been an art student in Stuttgart where he spent many hours drawing animals at the Nills Animals Show. Richard

designed a toy bear that was jointed in the same way that dolls are jointed; his toy bear could be dressed and played with in much the same way as a doll. Margarete was not impressed with the concept, but to please her nephew, she created a prototype of the toy bear and sent it to the Leipzig Trade Fair in 1903. While the bear received a lukewarm reception from most buyers, one enterprising American bought an original order of 3,000 pieces, which he soon doubled. By the end of the year, over 12,000 jointed Steiff bears had been shipped to the United States.

*These **Steiff** bears are 20 inches tall and made of mohair; they were manufactured around 1910.*

Clockwise from the top: These **Steiff** bears are Cinnamon Bear (13 inches tall, jointed, and stuffed with straw), White Bear (10 inches tall and fully jointed), Original Teddy (the smallest produced), Teddy Baby (3½ inches tall, made of mohair, and stuffed with straw), and Jackie Bear (7 inches tall and made in the U.S. zone of occupied Germany).

This **Steiff** bear was manufactured in occupied Germany after World War II and has a U.S. zone tag. He is jointed and made of mohair, with glass eyes.

This **Steiff** bear was manufactured around 1909; he is 16 inches tall and made of mohair.

Making, Selling, & Cuddling Teddy Bears

Teddy Bears: The Phenomenon Begins

President Roosevelt's decision not to shoot a bear, Clifford Berryman's cartoon, Morris and Rose Michtom's new product, and Margarete Steiff's willingness to go along with her nephew's idea wouldn't have mattered at all if hundreds of thousands of people in the United States had not suddenly decided that they absolutely had to have teddy bears. In the first decade of this century, a teddy-bear fad swept the country. People were willing to do practically anything to purchase teddies. It must have been very much like the Cabbage Patch Kid phenomenon of a few years ago, when riots broke out in toy stores that sold out of the dolls and some people were willing to pay outrageously high prices for Cabbage Patch Kids.

One large American toy store sold 60,000 teddy bears in 1906. The furniture industry was jeopardized because the mohair fabric needed to upholster sofas and chairs was being bought up to manufacture toy bears. The trade journal of the American toy industry, *Playthings,* reported record sales of teddy bears in 1906, describing the trend as "fairly rampant." *Playthings* went on to predict that teddies would have a "long and continued reign."

At first teddy bears were thought of as companions for boys, but it soon became clear that the little furry creatures had captured the hearts of young girls as well. The doll industry was concerned and quickly introduced teddy bears that wore clothes and could be bought with extensive wardrobes. It is equally clear that from the very beginning teddy bears were not just children's toys. Sweethearts gave each other bears, and college students adopted them as mascots. Photographs from the period show children of *all* ages clutching their favorite teddy bears.

By 1907 there were many companies making toy bears in both the United States and Europe. At first these companies simply called the stuffed bears "bruin" or "bear," but in 1906 the first trade ad for a bear named "Teddy Bear" appeared in *Playthings.* A Steiff ad from a 1907 issue of *Playthings* simply refers to their line of toy bears as "Genuine Steiff Bears." Other toy bears were known as Roosevelt Bears. A 1907 Columbia Teddy Bear Manufacturers' ad in *Playthings* reads, "Roosevelt Laughs and Shows His Teeth. . . . The Laughing Teddy Bear Laughs and Shows his Teeth at tight money, hard times, and pessimists." This open-mouthed bear, with his teeth bared, might not have been perceived to be as gentle as his stitched-mouth brothers if he had not been associated with the presi-

*This 10-inch **Steiff** bear is wearing his original outfit. He was shown in the company's 1924 catalog.*

*These two 12-inch **Steiff** bears were manufactured around 1908; they are made of mohair, stuffed with straw, and have shoe-button eyes.*

dent and described as being a laughing teddy bear.

Adding confusion to the debate about the origin of the teddy bear, a 1908 advertisement for the Ideal Novelty and Toy Company reads, "Our Bear is an exact reproduction of the foreign model." If Ideal was the originator of the teddy bear, why did the company use the word "reproduction" in its advertisement? Perhaps they were referring to jointed teddy bears, but who knows?

Once the teddy bear was firmly established as the toy everyone wanted to cuddle, bears began to take on all kinds of characteristics. Not content simply to make lovable, soft creatures, toy companies began to embellish

bears with every sort of gimmick imaginable. Old issues of *Playthings* are filled with advertisements for bears that do odd and unusual things. For example, an ad for Fast Black Skirt Company's Electric Bright Eye Teddy Bears claimed: "Shake the right paw, and the eyes light up with electricity in either white or red."

Musical bears were very popular. Bears with growlers, or voice boxes, inside them were in great demand, as were bears that tumbled and bears that were really dolls in bear suits. The fashion industry was unable to stay away from teddy bears. One children's clothes designer even created a fur outfit that made your child look like a polar-bear cub, and teddy-bear muffs were carried by fashionable little girls.

This **Steiff** bear has a blank button and was manufactured around 1904. He is made of curly mohair and stuffed with excelsior, and has jointed arms and legs and a swivel head.

This **Helvetic** bear was made in about 1920. She is 12 inches tall and has a music box.

This teddy bear was manufactured in the United States between 1915 and 1920.

This mohair teddy bear was made by **Ideal,** probably before 1910. He is 24 inches tall.

These **Steiff** bears were made between 1903 and 1910.

Teddy bears were adapted to become many different kinds of toys, including mechanical banks, pull toys, rocking bears, and bears on wheels, which could be pulled or ridden. Ads for teddy-bear carts and cages as well as children's chairs and rockers made by the Lloyd Manufacturing Company appeared in *Playthings* in 1907. That same year Sheldon and Kellers offered a rocking horse that was dubbed "the coming craze, the Teddy Horse." Perhaps the ad refers to Teddy Roosevelt, the equestrian, and not to teddy, the bear, since the toy looks very much like an ordinary rocking horse.

To understand the scope of the teddy-bear phenomenon, let's look at the sales figures of the leading German toymaker, Steiff. Keep in mind that, then as now, Steiff teddy bears were the most expensive as well as the most prestigious. In 1907, which Steiff called *Bärenjahre,* or "the year of the bear," the company sold a record one million teddy bears. In just four years since their introduction, teddy bears had become international best-sellers.

New and Improved Teddy Bears

Teddy bears have had their ups and downs since 1907. They struggled through the De-

This **Berg** teddy bear was made in 1946. Because of wartime shortages of materials, the bear was made with wool plush provided by the customer, and his growler is a match box filled with pebbles.

Galop-Teddy is a **Steiff** pull toy. When the wheels turn, one bear moves forward and the other backward alternately. Both bears are about 3 by 4 inches.

pression and survived two world wars. Early teddy bears were made of mohair, a fabric that resembles fur but is actually woven from goat hair. During wartime mohair was used to make warm uniforms for soldier, and other materials had to be found to make teddy bears. Felt, oilcloth, and rayon plush were substituted with varying degrees of success. Most of the early teddy bears had shoe-button eyes, but these were eventually replaced by glass eyes. More recently, manufacturers have begun using plastic safety eyes, which cannot be broken or injure small children.

*This **Steiff** bear is only 3½ inches tall. She was made in the 1930s.*

An interesting sidebar to the history of manufactured teddy bears is that no one bothered to register the trademark "Teddy" until 1987. Even though several people were involved in the original concept of a toy bear and more than a few people claim to have made the first teddy bear, no one registered the name itself. Today we often seem to prize a brand name more than the product it labels. Millions are spent to create a marketable item, such as Cabbage Patch Kids, that can be sublicensed to hundreds of companies to make thousands of related and unrelated items. These trademark names are often worth billions of dollars. But no one—not Steiff, Ideal, nor any one of the hundreds of other stuffed-toy companies—ever registered the name "Teddy Bear," until the North American Bear Co. obtained a trademark on the name "Teddy" for a toy bear.

German-Made Teddy Bears

The German toy company Steiff has made teddy bears that are consistently popular with both children and collectors. While other companies produce millions of stuffed bears, none has ever achieved the status that Steiff continues to hold. But Steiff is not the only German toy company that makes popular bears.

After World War II, the excelsior stuffing used by most bear manufacturers had to be replaced with washable polyester batting to conform to health and safety regulations. The laws governing toy safety have become stricter over the years, causing metal joints to be replaced first by wood and then by plastic. Dyes must be safe and nontoxic. Eyes and noses must have safety locks instead of being sewn on with thread that could break. These changes in regulations have helped to alter the appearance of teddy bears. Teddy bears used to be stiff, jointed toys stuffed with strawlike excelsior that made them feel hard until they had been hugged into softness. Most manufactured teddy bears are now soft, squeezable bears with floppy arms and legs.

*These twin Peter Bears were made by **Gebrüder Sussenguth** in 1925. They are about 14 inches tall and have wooden tongues. Their glass eyes roll back and forth when their tongues move.*

*Bellhop Bear (left) was made by **Schuco**; he's 15 inches tall. Second Hand Rose is 16 inches tall; she wears a real-fur boa and a felt hat with feathers, and carries a leather coin purse.*

head, a bottle cap is revealed. During the 1920s Schuco was best known for clockwork toys, but teddy bears were still an important part of their line. The company remained in business until 1970. Today Schuco miniature bears command high prices from collectors.

Other popular German-made teddy bears, which are still in production, are manufactured by Gebrüder Hermann KG. (The word *Gebrüder* means brothers.) The company began making teddy bears in 1907. Like Steiff bears, Hermann teddies have always been extremely popular in America, where they are sold in department and specialty stores. The teddy bears that Hermann makes today closely resemble the company's original bears; they have distinctive round faces and

*These three teddy bears were recently manufactured by **Hermann**.*

Schreyer and Company was founded in 1912 by Heinrich Schreyer and Heinrich Müller. While the company name is not too familiar, their trademark certainly is. Mention the name Schuco, and teddy-bear collectors will think you are talking about tiny teddies. Even though the Schuco trademark appeared on stuffed toys of every size, the company's little bears are their best-known product. These little teddies often measure only two and a half inches, but they are fully jointed with movable heads, arms, and legs. Some Schuco bears have yes-no mechanisms and shake their heads back and forth when you move their tails. Other Schuco bears are dressed as special characters, such as the bellhop bear. The company also made delightful perfume-bottle bears that have bottles hidden inside their bodies. When you remove the bear's short muzzles. This cute face distinguishes Hermann bears from most other German bears, which have longer noses and narrower faces. Hermann bears are fully jointed and made of the finest mohair. Like all the German manufacturing firms, Hermann suffered during the war years, and in 1948 the business relocated in the American zone of occupied Germany. You can identify a Hermann bear by the distinctive, bright-red, molded-plastic medallion on his chest with the large script inscription "Teddy."

*This **Hermann** teddy bear was made in about 1950. He is 11 inches tall.*

This **Hermann** teddy bear was made around 1920. She is 16 inches tall.

To celebrate its 75th anniversary, **Gebrüder Hermann** reproduced one of the company's original teddy bears. (The new bear is on the left.)

English-Made Teddy Bears

While most arctophiles debate whether the first teddy bear was made by Steiff or Ideal, a small group of teddy-bear historians supports the proposition that teddy bears originated in England. English bears are often named Edward, so they get nicknamed Teddy in the same way that American bears (and men) named Theodore are nicknamed Teddy. According to H.E. Bryant, the former director of Dean's Rag Book Company, Ltd., and Chairman of the British Toy Manufacturing Association, an Englishman invented the teddy bear. Bryant says that the British firm J.K. Farnell began making stuffed toys in 1897. While no documents have ever been produced to substantiate this claim, Farnell did make beautiful stuffed bears, many of which still exist. One of their most-popular lines of teddies is called Alpha Bears; these bears were designed by J.K. Farnell's sister Agnes and a toymaker named Sybil Kemp. Farnell bears often have labels sewn on their feet; these typically read "A Farnell Alpha Toy Made In England." There is some speculation that Christopher Robin's teddy bear, Winnie-the-Pooh, was a Farnell bear.

Chad Valley was one of the most-successful English companies that made teddy bears in the first part of this century. The company was founded in 1823, but the trade name Chad Valley was not used until 1919, when the company relocated by the stream Chad. During the 1920s Chad Valley acquired several other companies and expanded its toy production. The company manufactured many kinds of teddy bears, but the Chad Valley bears that seem to be most popular with collectors today are the ones with large, square-shaped, stitched noses. These bears have wide-spaced eyes and very sweet expressions, which are characteristic of English bears. In 1950 Chad Valley was sold by the family of the original owners and became a public company. During the 1960s the company expanded and had seven factories. In 1978 Chad Valley was purchased by Palitoy, a subsidiary of General Mills.

*This English bear was made by **Twyford** in the 1920s; he is fully jointed and made of mohair. The bear has glass eyes and an embroidered nose and mouth.*

Dean's Childsplay Toys, Ltd., is another English teddy-bear manufacturer. In 1903 Samuel Dean created Dean's Rag Book Company, Ltd., which was a subsidiary of Dean and Son, Ltd. Another subsidiary, Dean's Childsplay Toys, Ltd., was created in 1960. Dean's rag books were children's picture books printed on durable cloth. Since the books were washable, the company slogan was "These rag books are for children who wear their food and eat their clothes." Dean's also produced delightful printed-fabric toys that came on a sheet of fabric and had to be cut out and assembled at home. In 1912 Rag Knock-About Toy Sheets had many different designs, including dolls, puppets, and small animals.

named for Patricia Schoonmaker, a well-known doll collector and teddy-bear historian.

The two English toymakers that are currently very well known in the United States are Merrythought and the House of Nisbet. Merrythought, which uses an unbroken wishbone as its trademark, makes a popular bear named Cheeky. He's been around since 1955. Merrythought also makes plush versions of popular cartoon characters, including Donald Duck and Mickey Mouse.

In 1986 millions of people around the world were introduced to a Merrythought bear when the giant teddy found himself riding in the royal wedding carriage with Prince Andrew and his bride, Lady Sarah. The bear, festooned with pink and blue ribbons, was given to the Duke and Duchess of York by Prince Edward on their wedding day. In the spring of 1987, Merrythought began making a smaller version of the Wedding Bear so that teddy-bear collectors could share in the royal fun.

International broadcasts of royal events, such as weddings and coronations, were brand-new in 1953 when Peggy Nisbet, the founder of the House of Nisbet, created a portrait doll of Queen Elizabeth II in her coronation robes. Since that time the company has produced portrait dolls of many historical figures, but the House of Nisbet didn't begin making teddy bears until Jack Wilson joined the firm in 1977. He is married to Peggy Nisbet's daughter Alison, who worked with her mother for many years, creating an international market for the company's products. Soon after Jack Wilson joined the firm, he read Peter Bull's *The Teddy Bear Book* and decided to create Bully Bear in Peter Bull's honor. The House of Nisbet also makes a faithful reproduction of Delicatessen, Peter Bull's teddy bear that appeared in the television production of *Brideshead Revisited*. This wonderful re-creation even has worn fur and patches.

Elizabethan Bear is 14 inches tall; he was made by **Merrythought**.

Dean's had been making teddy bears for many years, but in 1920 the company introduced a series of bears and other animals on wheels. Continuing with the company tradition of whimsical slogans, these animals on wheels were advertised with this slogan: "It follows like a well-trained pet; all you have to do is pull the string."

Dean's produced a number of soft toys based on story-book characters, but their biggest leap into the American market came in 1930 when they became the first official manufacturers of stuffed-toy versions of Mickey Mouse and Minnie. Today Dean's Childsplay Toys continues to manufacturer fine teddy bears, including the Schoonmaker Bear that's

Continued on page 32

Four English teddy bears, made between 1930 and 1950, are seated in the front row. From left to right, they are 20 inches tall, 24 inches tall, 16 inches tall, and 18 inches tall. A **Schuco** bear that was made around 1960 stands in back.

The Bearington Family (Admiral, Victoria, and Baby) were made in England by **Merrythought***.*

Recently two more British companies have begun making teddy bears: Little Folk and the Canterbury Bear Company produce teddy bears of high quality that are likely to rank among the collectible teddy bears of the future.

American-Made Teddy Bears

For several generations the name Knickerbocker stood for fine soft dolls and stuffed animals. Like Merrythought and Dean's Childsplay Toys in England, the American-based Knickerbocker made stuffed toys that were based on Walt Disney characters. They also made Raggedy Ann and Andy, and more recently, Holly Hobbie dolls. Knickerbocker teddy bears have their own very special look. When Knickerbocker closed several years ago, the world lost a great toymaker.

While many of the first American teddy-bear manufacturers, including Ideal and Knickerbocker, have been disbanded, other firms are carrying on the tradition. Today the big names in teddy-bear manufacturing are Dakin, Gund, Russ Berrie and Company, Eden, Animal Fair, California Stuffed Toy, Applause, and North American Bear Co. Each of these companies has flourished as a direct result of a revival of interest in teddy bears.

North American Bear Co. is one of the most-popular and successful new American toymakers. The company makes colorful bears with names that pun the rich and famous. Barbara Isenberg is the founder and creative force behind North American Bear Co. She started out to create a special bear for her son and ended up making bears for millions of children and adults. From her snobby, rich bears, The Vanderbears, to her colorful V.I.B.s (Very Important Bears), you can see that Barbara Isenberg knows just which details are needed to complete each bear's character. Albert the Running Bear was one of her earliest character bears; he comes dressed in a jogging suit and running shoes. Albert has instant appeal for anyone who is pounding the pavement in hopes of attaining a higher degree of physical fitness. Albert even has his own line of books, including one on exercise.

While many American toy companies are part of larger corporations, a few new toymakers have revived the tradition of cottage toy industries. Bearly There is growing steadily, but it has kept its single focus. R. John Wright has gone from being a dollmaker to producing beautiful versions of Winnie-the-Pooh that are based on Ernest Shepard's illustrations.

This **Applause** *teddy bear isn't likely to lounge around the house all winter hibernating.*

*A 41-inch bisque doll takes her favorite pet animals for a walk. The doll was made in Germany in 1905. Her pets include a gray, curly mohair **Helvetic** teddy with a squeeze music box; a gold-colored 1930s **Steiff** bear; and a blank-button caramel-colored **Steiff** bear.*

Teddy Bears Rediscovered

If the first teddy was made in 1902, then the oldest teddy won't qualify officially as an antique until the year 2002. But teddy bears already sit alongside antique dolls and toys in prestigious auction houses and command prices that would normally be paid for objects far older and probably in better condition.

Teddy bears have also begun appearing in art galleries. The first gallery exhibition of new teddy bears was presented in New York in 1987. Dollmakers had worked for decades to achieve this kind of recognition for handmade dolls, but bearmakers found quick acceptance for their teddy bears as art objects, commanding the high prices usually associated with being shown in a New York gallery. At the first gallery exhibition, several bears sold for $1,500. A year later, bears made by the same artist were selling for twice that amount.

The continuing demand for old bears drives prices higher and higher, but the demand for teddy bears made by independent bearmakers is growing even faster, with prices climbing steadily. The current interest in teddy bears really got started in 1969 when the English character actor Peter Bull wrote a loving book about his teddy bears, which he entitled simply *The Teddy Bear Book*. Peter Bull had always been aware of the profound effect that teddy bears have on people. The subtitle of his book describes it as ''. . . the extraordinary effect he has had on men, women, and even children.''

Peter Bull was a fine actor; his range of characters went from the sublime to the ridiculous. He worked with many top stars, including Peter Sellers in *Dr. Strangelove* and Humphrey Bogart and Katharine Hepburn in *The African Queen.* Because of his reputation as an actor, Peter Bull may have found it rather disconcerting when he received a casting call not for himself but one of his teddy bears. When the producers of *Brideshead Revisited* were looking for a teddy bear to play the part of Aloysius, the beloved bear of Lord Sebastian Flyte, they called Peter Bull. After considering several bears, he selected one named Delicatessen. (Peter had given him this name because the bear spent his first 50 years sitting on a shelf in a food shop.) The enormous success of *Brideshead Revisited* both in England and later in the United States made Deli, or rather Aloysius, an overnight sensation. Delicatessen legally changed his name and officially became Aloysius. The whole business went to ''his dear furry head,'' according to Peter.

Peter Bull appeared many times on American television with his bears. He told their stories, talked about his book, and shared with a growing audience the good-hearted effect bears have on people. When people read Peter Bull's book or saw him on television, they realized that they were not alone in still loving their old teddy bears. All across the country, teddy bears were awakening from hibernation and coming down from attics and climbing out of trunks. The second phase of America's love affair with the teddy bear was about to begin.

Peter Bull's bear Delicatessen played the part of Aloysius in the television production of Brideshead Revisited.

In 1976 Janee and Howard McKinney opened the first store that sold teddy bears exclusively. Bears in the Wood in Los Gatos, California, has stood the test of time and is still one of the best teddy-bear stores in the United States. When the McKinneys opened their store, no one thought that they could sell enough bears to make a go of it, but they did. Today there are more than 300 teddy-bear stores in the United States.

In 1980 Barbara Wolters founded the *Teddy Tribune.* While this may not have been the first teddy-bear newspaper, it quickly became the most popular. Two years later Barbara hosted the first annual Teddy Tribune Convention in St. Paul, Minnesota. Her favorite bear, Dumper D. Dumper, was actually in charge of this premier American convention of arctophiles. British bear lovers had staged a mass rally in 1979. Reporting on the event, *Time* magazine used the headline "Arctophilia Runs Amok." But the convention in St. Paul was the first time American teddy-bear owners had gotten together.

Everyone attending the convention carried a favorite teddy bear. On the show day when the public was invited to come join the fun and see all sorts of fabulous teddy bears, several hundred people and their bears stood in the rain and waited to get inside. Local television stations covered the event, and before long teddy-bear shows and conventions were being held in many other parts of the country.

By the time Peggy and Alan Bialosky published *The Teddy Bear Catalog,* it was beginning to look as though bears were going to be the hot new collectible. The Bialoskys' book sent people climbing up into their attics and searching through their basements to check out their old teddy bears to see if they might be valuable to collectors. The book was

an instant best-seller, and soon everywhere you looked there were Bialosky posters, staonary, T-shirts, and aprons.

By 1986 there were twice as many toy companies making teddy bears as there had been three years earlier. Teddy-bear books, calendars, and notecards of all kinds were available. The *Teddy Bear and Friends Magazine* and *Teddy Bear Review* had begun publication and gained a subscriber base of more than 30,000 each. Ted Menten and other teddy-bear enthusiasts associated with *Teddy Bear Review* created the Golden Teddy Awards to honor handmade bears as well as the artistic excellence of commercially manufactured bears.

Making Teddy Bears at Home

Soon after teddy bears made their debut and found their way into the hearts of American families, people wanted to make their own teddy bears. The first teddy-bear patterns and kits appeared on the market in 1906. They gained immediate acceptance, as suggested by the December 1907 issue of *Ladies' Home Journal,* which has a full-page ad for teddy-bear clothing patterns. Printed sewing sheets were also available. These came ready to cut and sew; one 1906 issue cost only 35 cents.

Patterns for everything from teddy bears themselves to full lines of delightful outfits have been in print continually for more than 80 years. Today hundreds of patterns are available, including illustrated instructions in popular magazines and expensive kits produced under license from top designers.

Like rag dolls, teddy bears that are made at home often follow traditional designs. From year to year, they remain much the same as their ancestors. This was true of commercially manufactured bears as well. Only the keenest eye can detect the differences among early manufactured teddy bears. Like other traditional American crafts, teddy-bear making didn't change very much until recently.

*Bialosky is made by **Gund**.*

*This **Steiff** bear is 8½ inches tall; she was sold dressed, and only her head is jointed.*

*This 11-inch **Steiff** bear was made in about 1910.*

When teddy-bear lovers got together with their favorite bears ten years ago, the teddies were usually old family bears. Only a few people made bears, but many of these handmade teddies were exceptionally well crafted and quite beautiful. Arctophiles began asking bearmakers to sell their homemade teddies and soon a new industry was born.

Most of the first independent bearmakers lived on the west coast, primarily in northern California and Washington state. Beverly Port saw the potential of teddy bears. She was a popular dollmaker, and she struggled to make other dollmakers aware of teddy bears. Eventually a small community of bearmakers developed around Beverly Port. Word spread that wonderful handmade bears of very fine quality were being made, and other craftspeople began to make teddy bears. Most of these early bears were very traditional but not all of them. Beverly Port made teddy bears with porcelain faces and bears dressed as characters such as wizards and jesters. She made mechanical bears that rocked baby cubs in their arms. Beverly also made simple small bears that could live in an apron pocket and do all kinds of magical things.

By 1980 there were more than a dozen teddy-bear makers with established reputations for excellence. Their bears were sought after by a new group of teddy-bear collectors. Not all of these new bearmakers lived on the west coast. Doris and Terry Michaud were busy making bears in Michigan, and Marcia Sibol was hard at work in Delaware.

Teddy-bear conventions and shows were organized as collectors demanded an ever-increasing supply of new bears. By 1985 the number of bearmakers had doubled, and now there are more than 100 outstanding bearmakers who regularly show their bears.

Not all teddy bears are sold at teddy-bear shows; most are sold in small shops, and the people who own these shops have been a major impetus for the current popularity of

Just Ted was given to Terry and Doris Michaud by his owner. The fully jointed, 18-inch mohair bear was made in about 1924.

handmade teddy bears. These shopowners have encouraged bearmakers, advanced them money when it was needed, and educated their customers about what to look for in well-made teddy bears. Without the financial support and devoted encouragement from shop owners such as Joan Venturino, many important bearmakers might not have been able to keep on making bears. Joan produced the first full-color catalog entirely devoted to handmade teddy bears, expanding the market to people who live in parts of the country that cannot support a teddy-bear store.

*Beverly Port designed this clown bear for **Gorham**.*

Both teddy-bear artists and teddy-bear manufacturers have always made bears intended especially for collectors. But three years ago a major teddy-bear manufacturer decided to mass-produce bears designed by a well-known teddy-bear artist specifically for collectors. Gorham signed Beverly Port to create a "signature" line. Some bearmakers had been designing bears for toy companies, and others had increased their production output by hiring helpers and organizing cottage industries so that they had actually become small manufacturers. But Gorham was the first toy manufacturer to acknowledge a bearmaker's unique contribution to teddy-bear design and marketing.

Beverly Port's designs for Gorham include a full size and price range of bears in addition to decorative plates and music boxes. There is enough merchandise to allow a retailer to set up a Beverly Port display or create a Beverly Port corner. The concept has worked well, and in 1988 Gorham introduced a second complete Beverly Port collection.

Several other companies have signed well-known bearmakers to create bears for them. Merrythought acquired the rights to Chester Freeman's designs, and the House of Nisbet initiated a celebrity line of bears that features the work of several recognized teddy-bear artists, including Doris and Terry Michaud, and Carol-Lynn Rössel Waugh.

Some teddy-bear artists are concerned that the distinction between commercially manufactured teddy bears and handmade teddy bears is becoming blurred. These bearmakers would like to establish criteria to determine which teddies should be considered artist-made bears and which are commercially produced bears. Since any object signed by a celebrity has more value than an item not associated with a famous person, we can only imagine some time in the future when teddy-bear collectors will be trying to sort out which celebrity bears are which. Perhaps they'll use this book as a reference, but for now the question is purely academic.

In the past few years, teddy bears have changed considerably, as one bearmaker after another breaks with tradition and goes off in a new direction. While many bearmakers continue to work in traditional modes, others have taken whimsical leaps into entirely new realms of expression. More bearmakers, or teddy-bear artists as they are often called, are creating one-of-a-kind pieces instead of repeating a popular design. While this takes more creative energy and many additional hours of work, their bears are highly prized.

Famous Bears

Bears in the Woods

The bear in his natural habitat is both danger-
ous and ferocious. Giant grizzly bears can kill
a man with a single blow, but legend and
folklore tend to treat bears as benevolent
creatures. North American Indian legends, as
well as the European fairy tales collected by
Hans Christian Andersen and the Brothers
Grimm, only tell stories about good bears.
Walt Disney movies cast bears as basically
kind creatures, although Disney bears are occasionally dim-witted and bumbling. What is
there about these furry creatures that causes
humans to endow them with virtuous, loving
qualities?

Perhaps the answer lies in the fact that bear
cubs look like little children dressed in fur
suits. Their playfulness tends to make us think

they are harmless. Whatever the reason,
teddy bears have become an almost universal
symbol of tender, loving care.

Teddy-Bear Tales

The close association of President Roosevelt
with bears inspired writer Seymour Eaton to
create the Roosevelt Bears. Working with the
illustrator R.K. Culver, Eaton invented two
bears: Teddy B. and Teddy G. *The Roosevelt
Bears, Their Travels and Adventures* was published by Edward Stern in 1906, after appearing in Sunday newspaper supplements
as a full-page feature the year before. The
Roosevelt Bears are clearly not toy bears;
they're giant bruins from the Colorado
woods. They wander into civilization, dress in
human clothes, and easily mingle with
people.

Seymour Eaton has often been credited with
being first writer to use the name Teddy. Over
the years some people have assumed that
Teddy G. stood for Teddy Good, and Teddy
B., for Teddy Bad. Actually "G" stands for
gray and gay, and "B" stands for black and
brave. The Roosevelt Bears were very popular
at the time they were first in print; recently
they have resurfaced, and their adventures
are being reprinted. There are also several
stuffed-toy versions of these two lovable
big bears.

Teddy bears were a popular subject for books
around 1907, and a few of these books have
become children's classics, including *Denslow's Three Bears.* W.W. Denslow is best
known for his artwork in the *Wonderful
Wizard of Oz,* the first Oz book. Another classic, *Little Johnny and the Teddy Bears*, tells
"the uproarious adventures of six stuffed

*This Zotty Bear, which was produced by **Steiff** during the
1950s, resembles a real bear cub.*

*Like many literary bears, these two 3½-inch **Steiff** bears
(1920-1930) are setting off on an adventure. They've found
a place aboard Noah's ark.*

Teddy Bears who come to life by means of a wonderful elixir and with Johnny get into and out of all kinds of mischief." Johnny is a young boy who looks like Buster Brown. The illustrations are by J.R. Bray, and the ridiculous rhymes are credited to Robert D. Towne. *Little Johnny and the Teddy Bears* first appeared as a comic strip in the magazine *Judge.* Like many famous bears who were to come after them, these teddy bears appeared on several products, including silver cups and china plates.

L. Frank Baum and W. W. Denslow dissolved their partnership after the original Oz book was published. Both men claimed to have created the concept and both continued to do Oz stories. Baum's *Lost Princess of Oz,* published in 1917, has one of the first teddy-bear characters to appear in an Oz book. *Lost Prin-*

cess of Oz was illustrated by John R. Neill, who illustrated many Oz books but whose work has never been as popular as Denslow's. Some of Baum's other bear characters include the Lavender Bear King and his teddy named Pink Pinkerton, who has a key in his back and only tells the truth when the key is turned.

Bears Not Called Teddy

The basic, stuffed bear known as Teddy has always been and always will be the best-loved and most-popular bear, but the history of teddy bears would not be complete without telling the stories of some bears who were not named Teddy. The first of these legendary bears began appearing in the London *Daily Express* in 1920. He is a snow-white teddy bear called Rupert, who has been referred to as the British Mickey Mouse because of his enormous popularity. Rupert dresses in a red sweater with bright yellow-and-black-checkered trousers and scarf. He lives in a fantasy land called Nutwood, where he promotes law and order. Until recently Americans knew very little about Rupert, but now there are many Rupert products, including books and several stuffed-toy versions of this character.

In 1920 another legendary bear also began his career when Daphne Milne bought a bear at Harrods department store in London. The bear, then known as Edward (the traditional British name for toy bears), was a birthday gift for her then-one-year-old son, Christopher Robin. Edward soon became Christopher Robin's best friend and constant companion. His name was changed from Edward to Winnie, in honor of a real bear at the London Zoo, and to Pooh, for a swan that Christopher once knew. As Winnie-the-Pooh, this bear of "very little brain" had many exciting adventures with Christopher Robin and all his friends in

Tebro, an English toymaker, is licensed to manufacture Rupert. This bear is 25 inches tall, unjointed, and dressed in a red sweater and yellow-and-black-checkered trousers and scarf.

This pensive Pooh was designed by John Wright.

This unjointed Paddington bear, attired in a felt duffel coat, Wellingtons, and a rain hat, was manufactured by **Eden**.

entitled *Winnie the Pooh and The Honey Tree,* which was released in 1966. The Disney studio decided that Christopher Robin and his stuffed toys looked too British, so they were made to look more American. Sears obtained the product rights to the Disney version of Pooh, including stuffed toys. In 1984 Disney gave the right to make replicas of the original Winnie-the-Pooh to the American dollmaker R. John Wright.

A third British bear also found fame and fortune on both sides of the Atlantic. He came to life in 1956 when Michael Bond bought a bear for his wife at Christmas. Paddington, who is named after a British railroad station near Bond's home, traveled all the way from his native Peru only to find himself lost in London. He wears a floppy hat and a duffel coat with a large luggage tag hanging on one of the toggles that's inscribed, "Please look after this bear. Thank you."

Paddington is a charmingly muddled bear. He's much loved by children, and recently he's had his own animated series on British television and the HBO cable network. Many sizes and versions of Paddington are manufactured, including one by Eden Toys that has a music box and moves his head in time to the song.

More Literary Bears

American authors and illustrators have yet to invent a teddy bear with the universal appeal of Pooh or Paddington. Corduroy was created by Don Freeman in 1968; he is very popular with young children. Dare Wright, author of the popular children's book *Edith, The Lonely Doll,* wrote a book featuring two teddy bears in 1961. In *The Lonely Doll Learns a Lesson,* Edith is joined by a Schuco Yes-No Bear and a Steiff Jackie bear. The story is illustrated with photographs taken by the author.

My Circle of Bears by Michele Durkson Clise, with photographs by Marsha Burns, was pub-

the Hundred Acre Wood. The original Pooh and the other stuffed toys that once belonged to Christopher Robin now live happily in the children's reading room of the New York Public Library, where teddy-bear lovers of all ages can come and be properly awed by them.

A.A. Milne's first Pooh book appeared in 1926 and instantly became as popular with adults as it was with children. Like *Alice In Wonderland* and the *Wonderful Wizard of Oz, Winnie-the-Pooh* and *House at Pooh Corner* speak to children of all ages. The books were illustrated by Ernest Shepard, and for many years his delightful illustrations set the standard for all toy versions of Pooh and his friends.

In 1961 Walt Disney obtained the rights to the Pooh stories and produced an animated short lished in 1981. The bears in *My Circle of Bears* are a collection of antique teddies; most of them were made by Steiff. The charming stories and the sun-drenched photographs of the old bears surrounded by fresh flowers and antique props made this book an instant success.

In 1984 Michele Clise produced a second book, *Ophelia's World.* It tells the story of a snow-white bear named Ophelia who is a Parisian shop girl. The original Ophelia is a much-loved Steiff bear; her fur has been worn thin by hugs. Following the publication *Ophelia's World,* Steiff reproduced the original Ophelia in flawless detail so that all of her fans could have their own Ophelia. There are two more books in this series: *Ophelia's Voyage to Japan,* published in 1986, and *Ophelia's English Adventure,* published in 1987. To celebrate these books, Steiff created two new bears: Schnuffy, a bear dressed in a kimono from the Japanese adventure, and Baby Ophelia. Michele Clise clearly loves and understands bears, and her stories are written to be enjoyed by anyone who is young at heart.

Another wonderful old bear that captured the hearts of arctophiles everywhere is known as Bialosky. This old teddy is unusual because the book that made him famous was not meant for children. In 1980 Peggy and Alan Bialosky published *Teddy Bears, Pictures and Price Guidelines* (later revised and reissued as *The Teddy Bear Catalog*). This little book was intended to help teddy-bear collectors identify and appraise their old bears. There is nothing new or unusual about a price guide, but the Bialosky book had heart and soul, which is very special. So many people enjoyed the Bialosky book that Gund decided to manufacture teddy bears based on the old bear pictured on the cover of their book.

Another literary bear known as HUG came to life in plush after appearing in *The Teddy Bear Lovers Catalog,* which was also written for adult teddy-bear collectors. Like Rupert, HUG

Michele Durkson Clise's original Ophelia was a Steiff bear, and this replica of Ophelia is also made by **Steiff***.*

is a comic-strip character; he appears at the bottom of several pages of *The Teddy Bear Lovers Catalog.* Within a few weeks after the book was published, HUG received more than 5,000 fan letters from all parts of the United States. When the book was published in England and Japan, HUG began to get mail from all over the world. HUG's own book by Ten Menten, *The World According to HUG,* was published in 1984. Since 1987 HUG's comic strip has been a regular feature in *Teddy Bear Review* magazine. In 1984 North American Bear Co. produced the first plush version of HUG, and they also make HUG JR., BABY HUG, and HUG'S bear, Buddy.

A Talking Bear

Over the years there have been a few superstar toys, such as Barbie and the Cabbage Patch Kids. These kinds of dolls have endured well, becoming staple items of childhood. While the Cabbage Patch versions of teddy

bears, the Furskins, have not enjoyed the sensational response of the dolls, they too appear to be long-lived toys. But some heavily promoted bears, such as the CareBears, have come and gone without making much of an impact. One new teddy bear has startled everyone. His name is Teddy Ruxpin, and he can talk. Any arctophile or six-year-old child will tell you that *all* teddy bears can talk, but Teddy Ruxpin talks out loud.

In the few years since Teddy Ruxpin was introduced, he has survived his detractors and surpassed his imitators. He's a bear with charm. Teddy Ruxpin is special because he is *not* a traditional teddy bear. He doesn't appeal to collectors, but he has the qualities of traditional teddies that have made them collectible: He is charming and he is loving. Children growing up with Teddy Ruxpin will probably have the same feelings about their Teddy Ruxpins as people who grew up with Steiff bears have about their old teddies.

Teddy Ruxpin, the talking, animated teddy bear, was made by **Worlds of Wonder.**

Teddy, the Spokesbear

In the early 1900s just as today, teddy bears appeared in an array of forms made out of every possible material from paper to cast iron. If you can measure the popular appeal of teddy bears by how often they appear in advertisements for unrelated products, then teddy bears are right up there with pretty girls in bathing suits, selling everything from toothpaste to car radios. Leaf through any current magazine and see how often teddy bears are included somewhere in the ads; you'll find teddies used as props as well as premiums, logos, and spokesbears.

Teddy bears have been selling products and promoting causes and candidates for many years. Very soon after the first teddy bear was created, teddies helped their namesake win reelection as president. Theodore Roosevelt's

campaign buttons sported tiny stuffed bears hanging from them.

Newspapers and magazines have used teddy-bear paper dolls to encourage children to get their parents to buy their publications. Delightful teddy-bear paper dolls were printed in the *Boston Sunday Globe* in 1908, and *Pictorial Review* published "Ted E. Bear Goes A-Hunting" in 1909. The popular Dolly Dingle paper dolls also featured in *Pictorial Review* had a teddy-bear theme in 1924, when they featured a teddy-bear costume in "Dolly Dingle's Little Friend Joey Goes to a Carnival."

Teddy bears don't limit what they are willing to sell just to teddy-bear things. Teddies sell all kinds of regular, everyday products, like fabric softener and sandpaper. Recently a charming little bear named Snuggle has been acting as spokesbear for a fabric softener of

This Furskins hiker was made by **Coleco**.

the same name. A commercial version of Snuggle is produced under license by Russ Berrie and Company. During the 1940s the Behr-Manning Company advertised their sandpaper with a paper-doll bear named Barney. Their slogan read "Ask Daddy to use the sandpaper with the Barney in the Triangle." Barney looked more like a real bear than a teddy bear, but once he was dressed in one of his paper outfits, Barney could easily pass for a cuddly teddy bear.

One teddy-bear promotion for a California bank was actually too successful. Crocker Bank decided to offer a free teddy bear to every new customer who opened a checking or savings account. It seemed like a good idea at the time, but the *Wall Street Journal* reports that the teddy-bear incentive program misfired. New customers flocked to the bank to deposit money and take home a cuddly little bear, but when the bank's regular depositors also wanted bears, they were turned down. Hundreds of customers closed their existing accounts and opened new accounts so that they could get teddy bears. In desperation the bank finally canceled the promotion.

One of the most-touching examples of how a teddy bear helped to sell a concept is an ad run by the prestigious New York store Georg Jensen during the 1950s. The full-page ad in the *New York Times* shows a teddy bear wearing a black mourning arm band that is held together with a large pin. The bear is sitting all alone against a pure-white background. The bold headline over the teddy's head reads, "Some toys hate war." Underneath in smaller type, the copy explains that at Georg Jensen you would never find a toy that could teach your child to hate or kill.

*Snuggle is manufactured by **Russ Berrie and Company, Inc.***

*Smokey the Bear was first manufactured by **Ideal** in 1953.*

Smokey, the Noblest Bear of Them All

There are hundreds of teddies in literature and hundreds more associated with advertising promotions or television series, but there is one bear that is recognized by more people than all the others. Smokey the Bear was created in 1944, and he is reported to have a 98 percent recognition factor in the United States. Smokey was honored with a commemorative United States postage stamp in 1984 when he was 40 years old.

Like the legendary first teddy bear, Smokey's story is heroic. In 1941 forest fires in the United States had destroyed natural forests equivalent to the size of the state of Pennsylvania. Preventing fires became a major national concern. In 1942 the United States Forest Service launched a fire prevention campaign. Two years later the first Smokey the Bear appeared on a poster with the slogan

"Smokey says: Care will prevent 9 out of 10 forest fires." The original Smokey was drawn by Albert Staehle, who was a popular cover artist for the *Saturday Evening Post.* In Staehle's illustration, Smokey looks like a real bear with a long snout and a stern expression. Forest Service artist Rudy Wendelin created the Smokey that we are most familiar with. This softer, gentler version makes Smokey look more friendly. Wendelin continued to draw Smokey for 30 years.

Smokey the Bear first appeared as a stuffed toy in 1953, and he has remained in production continuously since then. The first Smokey bears were produced by the Ideal Toy Company. These teddy bears had molded, painted vinyl faces and paws, and soft stuffed, plush bodies. Smokey wore blue jeans and had a belt buckle with his name on it. He also wore a ranger's badge on his chest that was inscribed "Smokey/Ranger/Prevent Forest Fires." His ranger hat had "Smokey" printed on it. The Ideal Smokey carried a

shovel and came packaged with an official Junior Forest Ranger membership card, Smokey stamps with his picture, and a personal letter signed by the big bear himself.

The license to produce Smokey bears has been held by several companies after Ideal, notably Knickerbocker and Dakin. A true American hero, Smokey has taken his place in history beside Paul Bunyon, Pecos Bill, and Johnny Appleseed, as well as the original teddy bear.

Other Bears That Care

No other spokesbear has had the impact of Smokey the Bear, but there are other bears who are helping to save the environment and to make the world a better place to live. Determined Productions supports the World Wildlife Fund by contributing a percentage of their profit on the sale of teddy bears and other stuffed animals. Other bears promote a variety of worthwhile causes, and many teddy bears have been donated and sold to raise money for local and national charities.

*This teddy bear and panda were made by **Determined Productions** as part of the company's Wildlife Preservation Series.*

Some teddy bears are directly involved with helping people. Russell McLean of Lima, Ohio, became a local hero by visiting children in hospitals and bringing them teddy bears for comfort and solace. McLean brought bears and happiness to more than 60,000 children. Jim Ownby was inspired by McLean; he too wanted to make the world a better place. In 1973 Ownby founded Good Bears of the World. The organization has grown to include hundreds of bear dens in many parts of the world that collect money and teddy bears for sick and frightened children. Jim was a born salesman; he wouldn't hesitate to greet a total stranger with a bear hug and a "Good Bears" button just before he tapped him for a donation. Some people called Jim Papa Bear, but to his fellow Good Bears, Jim Ownby was always Bearo Number One.

Teddy bears have recently begun to be called upon to help more and more people—not just children in hospitals. Teddy bears are joining police forces to comfort lost, abused, and runaway children. Police departments in many parts of the country have teddy bears riding in their patrol cars to help officers deal with these youngsters. Back at the station house, other bears sit waiting to offer comfort to children under stress.

From the very beginning, teddy bears have delighted adults as well as children. The almost universal attraction of teddy bears is obvious. Human beings just seem to bond with teddy bears. We love the cuddly critters on sight and expect them to be our friends. Psychologists have known for a long time that people need to hold and be held (to hug and be hugged). One study has demonstrated the therapeutic effect of teddy bears on patients recovering from open-heart surgery. Patients often experience anxiety about coughing after the surgery. The fear of ripping open stitches can cause a patient to tense up and resist coughing. The study found that when patients clutched teddy bears to their chests over their stitches, their anxiety was relieved and they were able to cough more readily.

We may never understand the complex set of circumstances that enables a simple stuffed toy to provide so much comfort and joy. It may simply be enough that a teddy does. But the new role of teddy bears in hospitals and police stations is another testimony to the enduring love of teddy bears.

This **Little Folk** teddy bear, manufactured in the 1980s, brings love and joy with him wherever he goes.

Handmade Teddy Bears

Not very long after the first commercially manufactured teddy bears were adopted by American boys and girls, mothers and grandmothers in all parts of the United States began to make teddies at home. Patterns for bears and their clothes were sold through ladies' magazines and in dry-goods stores. Some people made teddy bears because they couldn't afford store-bought toys; other people crafted bears because they wanted to give a child or a friend a very special gift that was made with love.

Over the years other toys captured the hearts of American children, and teddy bears became less popular than they had been in the first decade of this century. Grown-ups went along with the children's new interests and sewed all kinds of stuffed toys and dolls, from Raggedy Ann to Cabbage Patch Kids. But during the 1960s and 1970s, as many people in the United States became interested in country crafts, nostalgic collectibles, and antiques, teddy bears started coming down out of attics and climbing onto rocking chairs and display shelves. These old, well-loved, and well-worn bears inspired a few people to try to make old-fashioned bears. By the early 1980s, about 20 people were making teddy bears to sell.

Gallery shows in New York, teddy-bear stores in California, and the publication of many new books about old teddy bears encouraged more and more people to make their own teddy bears. While many people make traditional teddies, many others now make teddy bears that are story-book characters, fairies, lawyers, doctors, pandas, or grizzlies. Almost any teddy bear imaginable is currently being produced by bearmakers, working alone or in small shops, in every part of the United States.

In the following pages, you will meet 100 of these teddy-bear artists. Their skill and dedication to their unique craft is evident in every teddy bear that these bearmakers produce. But teddy bears are more than toys or collectible objects; they are symbols of love and affection, and companions for hard times. Teddy bears share our secrets and encourage our dreams. Bearmakers know that teddy bears are important to people, and they include a little bit of themselves in every bear they make.

Shadow Chaser by **Ted Menten.**

53

Joanne Adams

Each Christmas morning of her childhood, Joanne Adams found a new doll under the tree. Her favorites were Ginny Dolls. Joanne liked to sew costumes for these little dolls, dressing Ginny as her favorite fairy-tale characters.

After Joanne became a teenager, she felt she was too old to play with dolls. She carefully packed her Ginnys in a suitcase. Joanne always kept the suitcase in the back of her closet, unable to part with this reminder of her childhood. Joanne didn't unpack her dolls again until her own children were almost teenagers. When she finally opened the suitcase, Joanne set free her childhood, realizing immediately how much she had loved and missed costuming dolls.

When Joanne began to make teddy bears, she experimented with several patterns until she developed her own design for a bear that's just about the same size as a Ginny Doll. Before long Joanne was turning these little bears into fairy-tale characters. Bearther Goose wears a flowing skirt so large that any number of bear children might be hiding under it waiting for a story. Little Bear Peep has found her sheep in Joanne's happy version of the tale.

Joanne retells the story of Little Bear Riding Hood in her own special style, complete with costumes and props. Little Bear is dressed in new boots and her best dirndl. The wolf has a big scary grin and seems ready to spring out of Grandmother's tiny bed at any moment. But this wolf is so charming, you just can't help but expect that everything will turn out all right.

Little Bear Peep is 8 inches tall and jointed; she is made of acrylic fur, is fully costumed, and comes with her sheep.

Bearther Goose is 8 inches tall and jointed; she is made of wool fur, is fully costumed, and comes with a plush goose and her wicker basket.

Little Bear Riding Hood is 8 inches tall and jointed; she is made of acrylic fur, is fully costumed, and comes with a basket, her grandmother's bed, and the wolf.

Durae Allen

Durae Allen makes teddy bears that just happen to look a lot like her. The bears have big dark eyes and an a special elegance and grace just like the aspiring actress who makes them. Durae became a bearmaker two years ago when she went to a teddy-bear show and found that she just couldn't resist the charm of the furry little creatures.

Durae makes many different kinds of teddy bears. They range in size from tiny one-inch bears to enormous four-foot bears. Some are dressed as ballerinas; others are Santas or jesters. Durae makes an old-fashioned fuzzy bear that is about three feet tall. Another bear is a king in an ermine cape. Durae even makes a little red devil bear with horns.

While she is working on a teddy bear, Durae waits and watches for the bear's character to evolve. When she was making the little bear that she now calls Lilly, it became apparent that the teddy was a young-girl bear. Durae knew immediately that Lilly's sweet, innocent face would look best if it were framed with a frilly hat and a fancy collar. Since Durae loves dressing teddy bears, she worked for a long time on Lilly's accessories until she got just the right look. "Nothing is worth doing if you don't put all your effort into it," Durae explains. Her careful attention to even the smallest detail and her use of the finest materials make Durae's teddy bears truly delightful.

Display Box Bear is 12 inches tall, seated; he is unjointed and made of synthetic fur.

Lilly in Her Hat Box is 12 inches tall and jointed; she is made of mohair and wears a hat, a lace collar, and a bow.

Darci & Scott Andrews

In a small winery in California's Napa Valley, they're making more than wine. Darci and Scott Andrews are making teddy bears at the Bear Cellar Winery. They've set up sewing machines and cutting tables next to the oak vats and grape-crushing equipment. But to keep the bears from feeling out of place, the Andrews name them after wines—Pinot Blanc, Barbeara, Johannesburg Riesling, and Burgundy.

Black Barbeara is a gentle teddy bear, named for the sweetest wine grape. Blanc de Blanc is a playful polar bear that can sometimes be seen poking his head from around a vat. Carnelian has a look of wonder and innocence about his eyes, as well he might since he's named for a new grape developed in California. In the tasting-and-hugging room at Bear Cellar Winery, you'll also see Sparkling Wine Teddy. His fur is tipped with the color of pale frost so he looks as bubbly as a glass of champagne.

Winegrowers like to experiment, and so do bearmakers. Darci Andrews hasn't been content to limit her designs to only a few kinds of bears. She also makes a panda called Ping and a bear with a truly unique coat called Bentley. He's made out of the fabric upholstery from Bear Cellar Winery's 1931 Bentley.

Some years are better for wine than others, but every year is good for the teddy bears made at Bear Cellar. Their characters and expressions may be a little different from time to time, but the essential teddy bear always comes through.

Ping is 12 inches tall and jointed; he is made of plush, has a ribbon tie, and holds a pair of chopsticks (not shown).

Carnelian (left) is 18 inches tall and jointed; he is made of European plush, has a ribbon tie, and comes with a wooden wagon filled with plastic grapes (not shown). *Black Barbeara* (right) is 16 inches tall and jointed; she is made of plush, wears a pleated collar, and comes with a cork and a grapevine wreath (not shown).

Celia Baham

After school Celia Baham used to visit her mother in the factory where she worked as a seamstress. Her mother and the other seamstresses taught Celia how to make patterns and cut different kinds of fabric. She also learned to sew on a large, industrial sewing machine. Today Celia uses these skills to make exquisitely dressed teddy bears.

Celia charges each of her bears with helping the people he meets to feel happy. Before a teddy bear leaves her workshop, Celia makes sure that the teddy conveys warmth and caring. After Celia finished sewing Bearnocchio, she stepped back to look at him. But there was something wrong. The little bear looked lonely in a way that made Celia feel very sad. It's all right for a teddy to seem to be lonely if he also looks like he's just waiting for you to come along and pick him up. But Bearnocchio looked relentlessly lonely, so Celia thought for a moment and came up with the idea of giving him a teddy-bear puppet to play with. The marionette Strings was just what Bearnocchio needed; he now has a sparkle in his eye.

Celia makes Carousel Horse with Clown Bear riding on its saddle. She uses a welded armature for the horse that she makes herself; welding is just another of Celia's many craft skills. Celia also makes a bear family. Dressed in their best clothes and polished leather shoes, they look as though they are about to go out for a Sunday-afternoon stroll through the park.

Precilla is 18 inches tall and jointed; she is made of mohair and wears a cotton dress trimmed with eyelet, an embroidered collar, and a straw hat.

Honey Creme is 23 inches tall and jointed; she is made of plush, has glass eyes, and wears cotton clothes and a straw hat, trimmed with satin and silk flowers. Her *Cubs* are 12 inches tall and jointed; they are made of wool coat fabric, and wear handmade cotton clothes and real leather baby shoes.

Bearnocchio is 21 inches tall and jointed; he is made of mohair and wears velour and cotton clothes, a felt hat with a feather, and satin bow tie. *Strings* (the marionette) is 10 inches tall and loose jointed; he is made of wool.

Carousel Horse is 12 inches long from his nose to his tail; he is made of wool felt, with a rabbit-fur mane and tail. *Clown Bear* is 8 inches tall and fully jointed; he is made of wool, has glass eyes, and wears a lamé costume.

Reneé Koch Bane

Not all bearmakers grew up clutching grubby, well-loved teddy bears. Reneé Koch Bane can't remember having a teddy when she was a child. She's not even sure exactly how she got started making bears as an adult. Reneé had been busily sewing costumes for a little-theatre group when she came across a pattern for a classic teddy bear. For some reason she felt that she simply had to try to make that bear. It was love at first stitch. After Reneé had made one bear, she just couldn't stop and has gone on to develop at least a dozen different bear designs and to make hundreds of teddies.

Reneé enjoys making bears, but she likes sharing her teddy bears with collectors even more. She knows how happy her bears make people. Who can resist any of the Sociable Bears, as Reneé calls her teddies. Standing Baby Bear—her favorite cub—stands tall on his own two feet and reaches his arms out to you for a hug. The Mischief Teddies romp through the world always on the lookout for fun and honey. The Canterbeary Bears are soft and sweet. The Black Forest Bear is a delightful cub that seems to have left his den in the woods to come to your house for tea and honey cakes, and decided to stay on in your comfortable, warm home.

Reneé makes bears in many colors and sizes, but all her teddies are easy to fall in love with. Reneé has more than made up for all the bear hugs she missed as a child.

Canterbeary Bears are 12 inches tall and jointed; they are made of German plush and wear bows.

Standing Baby Bear is 15 inches tall and jointed; he's made of German plush.

Black Forest Bear is 10 inches tall and jointed; he's made of German plush.

Mischief Teddies are 12 inches tall and jointed; they're made of mohair.

Jody Battaglia

Jody Battaglia makes teddy bears that tell stories. Some of them tell bear versions of familiar nursery rhymes and fairy tales; other teddies have their own tales to tell. Her Little Bo Peep has lost her sheep, but she doesn't seem to be too worried. She knows her lambs are bound to be back soon. Pinocchio has an ordinary bear nose, rather than a long nose, because Jody believes that teddy bears can't lie. Obviously Jody has a very high regard for teddies, and she says none of them has ever let her down.

Little Red Riding Hood was designed not only to carry a basket of goodies to her own grandmother but also to carry good wishes to ailing human friends and relatives. Riding Hood is not the only one of Jody's bears that's likely to be sent to a sick friend. Robbie is a football-player bear that broke his leg during the homecoming game. Two other indisposed bears, Marjorie and Martin, seem to have just a touch of flu, or perhaps they only want to stay home and shuffle around the house in their bunny slippers.

Jody's teddy bear Theodore is an innocent little hero that's a friend to both bears and people. Like all of Jody's bears, he seems to be a child playing dress up. He looks up into your eyes in a mischievous way that encourages even the most serious, grown-up person to smile.

Theodore *is 6 inches tall and jointed; he is made of acrylic fur and wears a military uniform, Roughrider hat, and glasses.*

Little Red Riding Hood *is 9 inches tall and jointed; she is made of acrylic fur, has glass eyes, and wears a cotton dress, apron, pantaloons, and hooded cape.*

Pinocchio is 9 inches tall and jointed; he is made of acrylic fur and wears cotton shorts, suspenders, and shirt, and a felt hat with a feather.

Little Bo Peep is 9 inches tall and jointed; she is made of acrylic fur and wears a cotton dress, apron, pantaloons, and bonnet.

Doris Beck

Miss America Bear is 16 inches tall and jointed; she is made of distressed mohair, has Ultrasuede paws and glass eyes, and wears a velvet cape, a satin sash, and a rhinestone tiara and earrings.

Doris Beck started out making tiny teddy bears for her antique dolls to hold. But before she knew what was happening, she found herself becoming a serious, full-time bear-maker. While she was still an amateur, Doris displayed her work at the Washington State Fair and won a blue ribbon. Then a friend put Doris's bears in the window of her store, and orders for more bears than Doris had ever dreamed that she could make came pouring in. She decided to call her enterprise Dori's Bears and set about filling those first orders, as well as the hundreds of new orders for teddies that have continued to come in.

Doris finds the inspiration for her teddy bears in her own childhood memories. Her bear Humphrey is a large bear with a sincere face; he's the kind of bear Doris can remember cuddling up with while she read a good story. Cozy Bear is like the soft rag dolls Doris played with when she was a child. The bear's floppy body hugs you close, and her blue eyes look at you with unconditional love.

Doris's Miss America Bear may be a home-town bear that's made it to the top, or she may be a sophisticated city bear that's always gotten exactly what she wanted. It's hard to tell because this bear is definitely enjoying her moment of glory. She waves to her admirers and graciously thanks them for their support.

Humphrey is 22 inches tall and jointed; he is made of mohair, has Ultrasuede paws and glass eyes, and wears only a ribbon.

Catherine Bordi

Friend Bear is 12 inches tall and jointed; he's made of camel's hair.

Catherine Bordi had always been curious about how a teddy bear was jointed. After she saw an X ray of an antique bear and discovered that its joints were simple arrangements of washers and cotter pins, Catherine couldn't wait to try to make a teddy bear on her own. Finding just the right hardware and materials held her back for a while, but she was soon manufacturing and selling her Chocolate Bears. Actually Catherine left the marketing of her bears to a teddy she calls her Little Salesman. His looks are so appealing that, when she took him along on sales calls, shopowners invariably wanted to buy him. When they couldn't buy him, there was nothing for them to do except to place an order with Catherine for other teddy bears.

The Pinecone Forest Bears are Catherine's favorite teddies. She designed this bear several years ago, but even though she's made hundreds of them, Catherine has never found a way to improve on her original design—a classic teddy with long arms and a humped back, made of soft German plush.

Catherine's bears are made to be loved; she expects people to talk to her teddies and to confide in them. She knows that her little bears will reflect back wisdom and serenity. A good teddy bear has a look in his eyes that tells his owner just how special he or she truly is.

Bottom row from left to right: *Grizzled Brown Bear* (15 inches), *Pinecone Forest Bear* (14 inches), and *Pinecone Forest Bear* (18 inches). Top row from left to right: *Friend Bear* (12 inches), *Dark Grey Antique Style* (13 inches), and *My Little Salesman* (13 inches). They are made from synthetic fur and are fully jointed.

Pinecone Forest Bear is 18 inches tall and jointed; he's made of European acrylic fur.

Two **Pinecone Forest Bears:** They are 18 inches tall, fully jointed, and made of acrylic fur.

An 18-inch **Pinecone Forest Bear.**

Several years ago, Loretta Botta found a pattern for a teddy bear in an antique shop. She decided to try her hand at making bears, and before long Loretta was turning out one beautiful teddy bear after another. She gave her first Botta Bears distinctive printed paw pads, and this continues to be Loretta's trademark.

Loretta's mother, Lilly, not only designs and makes clothes for the teddy bears, but she also showed Loretta how to make jointed bears. Lilly remembered the small, jointed German teddy bear that she had when she was a child; she figured out the way his joints had worked and explained it to Loretta. The clothes that Lilly makes for the bears are often very elaborate, and she will even make shoes when she feels they are necessary to complete a teddy bear's outfit. Lilly dresses Loretta's jester bears in bright tunics and pointed shoes, and she made a marvelous ball gown for the elegant bear Mademoiselle Leonie Deveraux.

Allister is 24 inches tall and jointed; he is made of acrylic fur, and has Ultrasuede paws and a yarn nose. The photographer provided the costume and props.

Allister is one of the largest bears Loretta has ever made. He often rides around with her in the front seat of her Morris Minor. The big bear looks even bigger in such a tiny car. Allister's cousin, Theo, almost spent his first Christmas as a store-window decoration, but he looked so sad when the shopowner was closing her store on Christmas Eve that she took him home for the holiday. He decided to stay and has been part of her family ever since.

Mademoiselle Leonie Deveraux is 14½ inches tall and jointed; she is made of acrylic fur, wears a satin gown trimmed in lace and roses, a hoopskirt, and a pearl-and-rhinestone tiara, and carries a flirting fan.

Mary Ellen Brandt

When Mary Ellen Brandt's aunt gave her several old fur coats, Mary Ellen made an unusual choice about what she wanted to do with the them: She decided to make teddy bears. One of Mary Ellen's friends is a dollmaker, and she suggested that Mary Ellen use the coats to make stuffed animals. Mary Ellen's first real-fur animal was an elephant. But the second animal she made was a teddy bear. He was inspired by her first teddy, which Mary Ellen has kept with her since she was five years old. The first real-fur bear was a great success, and Mary Ellen has been making very elegant teddies out of recycled fur coats and stoles ever since.

Mary Ellen often uses fur from two or three coats or fur pieces to make one bear. A combination of different furs creates the special effect Mary Ellen is looking for in her teddy bears. To show off the fur to its best advantage, Mary Ellen doesn't costume her bears. She uses molded plastic noses because needle-work noses might pull out the fur.

Mary Ellen's bear Reynard is made from red fox and Japanese mink. He's rather shy and not the least bit crafty. Her teddy bear named Brooke is made of white and autumn-haze mink; he looks like a fanciful version of his cousin Mae Lee, the panda. Mary Ellen's pandas are made of Norwegian blue fox and other dyed furs, such as opossum, mink, fox, or skunk.

Reynard (two shown) is 15 inches tall and jointed; he is made of red fox and Japanese mink, and wears a satin ribbon bow.

Brooke is 12 inches tall and jointed; he is made of autumn-haze and white mink, and wears a bow.

Deanna Brittsan

While Deanna Brittsan is making a teddy bear, she imagines what the bear's life might be like. Her bear Miss Prudence Plum is a school teacher in a small town. Billy Furman is one of Miss Plum's pupils; he spends a lot of time standing in the corner because he just can't help being mischievous. Clarence Beuford is a traveling salesbear that happens to run into Prudence one morning when she is speeding down the sidewalk on her way to the dry-goods store. Deanna can imagine that this chance meeting may lead to a romance between the two bears. Perhaps they'll even marry, raise some cubby bears, and move to another town.

Ever since she was a girl, Deanna has been inventing stories and making wonderful things out of practically nothing. She has always sewed and began making teddy bears when she found a pattern in a magazine. Deanna soon developed her own designs, and she often combines seemingly disparate concepts with terrific results. Her teddy Duck Soup, for example, began with a cotton print fabric that has a duck motif. Deanna decided that a bear that would wear a playsuit with ducks all over it would also want duck slippers, so she made a bear with a playsuit and slippers, and named her Duck Soup. Deanna can also be inspired by an old doll's dress or even a dress that once fitted a child to make a bear. She'll make a teddy bear to fit the dress. One of Deanna's teddies, Little Lucy, proudly wears a hand-me-down party dress.

Miss Prudence Plum is 17 inches tall and jointed; she is made of mohair and wears a skirt, a blouse, a lace collar, and a straw hat.

Pebbles is 13 inches tall and jointed; he is made of mohair and filled with beans.

Deanna Brittsan

Duck Soup *(two shown) is 13 inches tall and jointed; she is made of synthetic fur and wears a hat, a playsuit, and wool-felt duck slippers.*

Genie Buttitta's teddy bears are definitely characters. To get just the right expression on a bear's face, Genie often remakes the face three or four times, carefully sculpting and shaping until the teddy becomes exactly the bear Genie had intended to make. Each Buttitta bear has a name, and many wear elaborate costumes or come with props, so you'll know exactly who they are and what part they are to play in your life.

Hoakey is a backwoods kind of bear; he comes with a carved wooden fish that reminds him of the many happy hours he's spent sitting beside a stream, thinking his own thoughts, and waiting for a fish to bite. The Peddler wears a brocade cloak and carries a wooden tray filled with all kinds of tempting wares from candlesticks to sewing thimbles and fine lace. Red Bearon dons his goggles, helmet, and flight jacket, and prepares to fly his plane wherever duty calls.

Of all Genie's bears, Julius C. Bearmaker is perhaps the closest to her heart. "He can do everything," she says of this distinguished gray bear that peers over his glasses at the tiny teddy bear he's stitching up. His workbench is cluttered with fabric and partially finished bears much like Genie's own sewing table. Also like her, Julius is a thoughtful bearmaker; he puts a little of himself into every character he creates.

Red Bearon is 8 inches tall and jointed; he is made of acrylic fur and wears an imitation-leather jacket, helmet, and goggles. He comes with a wicker plane (not shown).

Julius C. Bearmaker is 17 inches tall and jointed; he is made of imitation Persian lamb and wears a shirt, a tie, a vest, and a leather apron. He comes with a stool and a workbench, which includes three small teddy bears, a pin cushion, and scissors.

The Peddler is 14 inches tall and jointed; she is made of mohair, wears a brocade cape, and comes with a wooden tray and a backpack fitted out with an assortment of miniatures and notions.

Hoakey is 17½ inches tall and jointed; he is made of acrylic fur and comes with a wooden fish (not shown).

Pam Carlson

On Christmas Eve, 1982, Alexander A. Bear sat under the tree at the Carlsons' home in Oregon. He was the first teddy bear that Pam Carlson had ever made, and he was something of a miracle. For much of her life, Pam had worked with a sewing needle or a paint brush in her hand, but multiple sclerosis made it impossible for Pam to go on making the crafts she loved. For several years she sat idle, but that year as Christmas approached, Pam decided she had to make something to put under the tree. A teddy bear shaped itself in her mind; slowly and painfully she got to work. As the bear took form, Pam began to feel stronger.

After Christmas Pam was feeling so much better that she decided to help her family at a wholesale gift show. She took Alexander Bear along just to keep her company, but before the show was over, Pam had orders for 400 bears. Making one bear had been difficult for her, so Pam called up just about everyone she knew to come and help her fill the orders.

Pam's company, A Bear and Friends, has made many bears since then. The loving spirit of the friends and family who work together to make the teddies carries over into the bears. All of Pam's bears look like family. As the business has grown, Pam's strength has increased, and she now makes all the bears herself. In addition to bear making, she's become a guidance counselor and often uses her bears to help hurt people heal. Pam certainly understands how much difference a teddy bear can make in someone's life.

Andrew is 4 inches tall and jointed; he is made of mohair and wears a sweater.

Ashton A. Bear and *Abigail Bear* are 10 inches tall; *Alison* is 7 inches tall, and *Amy* is 4 inches tall. They are jointed, made of mohair, and dressed in handmade clothes.

Pat Carriker makes small bears and tiny bears in a studio she had built on to her house. Her workshop is a cozy room with a skylight and a wood stove. There's a sitting area for friends who stop by to visit and lots of small furniture and other things that teddies enjoy. Pat's small bears (the largest one is about five inches tall) are a family of four. They like to sit on a dollhouse sofa, which makes them look as though they were about to have a formal portrait made. Some miniature bears enjoy hanging out on the steps of a tiny gazebo; others take Pat's mechanical model of a 1956 Thunderbird out for a spin.

Pat's two-and-one-half-inch teddy bears can be—and are—almost anything. Some are dressed as children in vests, sweaters, or sailor suits, but many wear costumes. Pat makes bears that look like they're ready to go out for trick or treat: They're dressed as witches, clowns, ballerinas, strawberries, Indians, cowboys, clowns, hobos, and pumpkins. There's Santa and Mrs. Claus, a train engineer, and a fairy. Pat even makes a bride and groom; they've often been called upon to take a place of honor on top of a wedding cake.

The well-dressed family of four teddy bears always leaves Pat's studio together. Mom wears a picture hat; Dad has a frock coat. Brother wears a sports cap, but he hasn't outgrown his knitted playsuit. Baby is dressed in white lace. The Family would be at home in any well-appointed dollhouse.

The **Family** are jointed bears that are made of cotton velour. **Dad** is 5½ inches; **Mom** is 4½ inches; **Brother** is 4 inches, and **Baby** is 2½ inches.

Left to right: **Baby in PJs, Strawberry, Shopper, Clown, Witch, Pumpkin Bear, Rabbit, Engineer, Lady in Boa,** and **Fairy** (on top of gazebo). They are 2½ inches tall and jointed.

Lynda Carswell

Emily's Christmas Bear (left) and **Heirloom Bear** (right) are 13 inches tall and jointed; they are made of European acrylic and wear hand-knitted sweaters.

Lynda Carswell makes traditional teddy bears. She works nights as a nurse, but during the day while her children play around the house, Lynda designs and sews her Heirloom Bears. They are made of many colors of plush, and some of the teddies wear bright-red hand-knitted sweaters. All of Lynda's bears can stand on their hind legs and on all fours like real bears. Her bears can also surprise you with a well-executed headstand. Black Bear is especially adept at this trick.

Lynda was a professional bearmaker before her children were born. But in spite of the increasing popularity of her bears, she still found time to make each of her three children his or her own special bear. Her daughter Emily's one-of-a-kind bear is made of European plush. Lynda found a sample of the fabric and hoped to order more, but she was never able to get any, so she made Emily's Christmas Bear from the sample. Lynda's sons, Jeremy and Christopher, also have their own bears. Like all of Lynda's bears, they have safety eyes so that they can be held and cuddled by children as well as grown-ups.

Lynda has been making teddy bears for about 15 years, and she says she never gets tired of watching a person fall in love with one of her bears. There's no way to predict which teddy will have just what it takes to pull a person toward him. But when a teddy bear finds his true owner, he is sure to convince you to take him home.

Heirloom Bear is 15 inches tall and jointed; he is made of European acrylic and wears a hand-knitted sweater and cap.

Deri Cartier

Each year more than 3,000 of Deri Cartier's huggable teddies leave Washougal, Washington, to go out into the world. Like many other bearmakers, Deri works in the basement of her house. But unlike bearmakers who limit their production to a few bears, Deri decided that if she was going to make charming and delightful teddies, she wanted them to charm and delight as many people as possible. While most Cartier Bears are handmade, they are not one-of-a-kind showpieces. They are made to love and have safety eyes and noses, and strong appliqué stitching on their paws.

Big Snowy is as soft as new snow. She curves her arms around you when you hug her in a way that lets you know that she's stuffed with love. Little Chocolate Chip is so yummy he'll melt your heart. His little paw pads look just like dollops of chocolate. Each of the other Cartier Bears also has his or her special charm, but all of them, except the jointed bears, have floppy arms and legs so that they always hug you back whenever you hug them.

When Deri first began to design teddy bears, she thought about the animals she'd seen in the zoo. She realized that "no one wants a bear that looks like the real thing. Bears have big teeth and little, mean eyes and long, sharp claws." Deri decided to forgo realism and give her teddy bears the things about a bear that people love—"the fuzzy hair and the great round bodies."

Elizabeth Ann is 10 inches tall and fully jointed; she is made of fake fur and wears a lace collar with a ribbon rosette.

Little Chocolate Chip is 17 inches tall and unjointed; he is made of high-quality fake fur and wears a ribbon bow.

Carol Cavallaro

Beasley is 15 inches tall and jointed; he's made of mohair.

When Carol Cavallaro was a year and a half old, she was adopted. Her new mother was a nurse who lived in New York. She knew that her little daughter would need a special companion to help her get through the long days and longer nights, so Carol's mom bought her a teddy bear. She called the bear Pooh, and he was her first and best friend.

Pooh went everywhere with Carol. They visited Dr. Benjamin Spock, who was a friend of Carol's mother, and went shopping at Saks Fifth Avenue and Bonwit Teller. But Pooh was often naughty; he would get lost, and Carol and her mother would have to search high and low for the little golden bear. Somehow they always managed to find him.

Carol made her first teddy bear when her mother became very ill and had to leave her home. Just as 40 years earlier Pooh had comforted the little girl in her new home, Carol's first teddy became her elderly mother's constant companion.

Of all the teddies she makes, Carol's favorite bear is still a shaggy-haired, golden bear. She calls him Beasley. He's a mischief maker with a sunny face. Like Pooh, Beasley is always up to something just a little bit naughty. Carol also makes a little silver bear with kind eyes and a ragamuffin bear called Marshall. To make sure he doesn't get lost, she puts a bell on the ribbon around his neck.

Silver is 15 inches tall and jointed; she is made of alpaca and wears a cotton pinafore and ribbons.

Barbara Conley & Tracey Roe

Barbara Conley set a course toward becoming a bearmaker when she bought a Victorian house and decided to fill it with antiques. While she was buying furniture, she bought an old doll to sit in a chair that just didn't look right empty. But the doll was lonely so Barbara brought home more dolls. Then the dolls needed something to play with so Barbara began to buy Steiff animals. Finally she bought two old teddy bears, and soon Barbara attempted to make a bear of her own design.

Barbara started the Roley Bear Company with her daughter, Tracey Roe. The two women don't make teddy bears in the same studio; each one works in her own home in different cities. But it's impossible to distinguish the bears Barbara makes from the ones Tracey makes because all Roley Bears have classic features and a special look in their eyes that pulls at your heartstrings.

For these bearmakers shaping the teddy's face is the most important part of the process of crafting a bear. They have made hundreds of beautiful teddy bears, but they have yet to make a teddy that they consider to have a perfect face. To less discriminating eyes, their bears Edward and January seem to have exactly the look a teddy bear should have. Edward has a slight smile on his face that lets you know that he's a teddy bear you can trust. January is a hauntingly beautiful bear that reaches out his long arms and waits for you to pick him up.

January is 24 inches tall and jointed; he's made of mohair.

Edward is 20 inches tall and jointed; he is made of mohair and wears a collar, a bow tie, and a tuxedo shirtfront.

102

Cindy Coombs

Whenever Cindy Coombs went to visit her grandparents in the country, she couldn't wait to go upstairs to her mother's childhood room and hug her mom's old, worn-out teddy bear. Cindy is a mother now herself. She lives in the country, and that well-loved teddy is her proudest possession. He was the inspiration for the first teddy bear Cindy made when she was ten, and he continues to inspire Cindy and her bear-making students today.

Cindy's first teddy was made of black plush and had big, funny ears. Cindy says he really looks a lot more like a mouse than a real teddy bear. Carrying on the family tradition, Cindy's son cherishes his mom's first bear. He hates it when she borrows the bear to take him to one of her classes. Cindy uses her mousy teddy to show her students that great bears can come from humble beginnings.

Cindy makes plain, lovable teddy bears that seem to tell a story simply with their expressions. Lavender is mischievous; she may look innocent, but you can be sure that she's always dreaming up her next adventure. Gretchen looks like she's just about to break into giggles over some new joke. Jo Jo is a little sweetheart, but you know she's likely to slip down off your lap to go romp through the woods. Justy, short for Just Pokin' Fun, is something of a clown. He's sure to make you laugh with his little puppet.

Gretchen (left) is 13½ inches tall and jointed; she is made of English mohair, wears a straw hat and satin ribbons, and has a music box. *Lavender* (right) is 9½ inches tall and jointed; she is made of mohair and wears silk flowers around her neck.

Justy is 15½ inches tall and jointed; he's made of English mohair, dyed to create a motley. He wears a jester's cap, carries a puppet, and has a music box.

Candy Corvari

Candy Corvari's grandparents lived in a log cabin in the mountains of Washington. She often stayed with them, and one of her favorite childhood memories is of going with her grandfather to a clearing in the woods to watch a big bear and her cub feed on wild berries. Candy often thinks about those real bears while she's making teddy bears, but she has never tried to make realistic bears. Candy usually makes classic teddy bears, although recently she has been designing teddies with jointed knees so that the bears can be posed to look as though they are running and playing. Her bear Boy with Kite races forward to catch the wind, and a girl bear in a crisp white Victorian dress sits properly on a chair with her knees bent and her feet on the floor.

Candy made her first bear while she was living in St. Louis. She was homesick for the mountain forests and housebound with a newborn baby. To cheer her up, Candy's mother came up with the idea that she ought to make a teddy bear for her little son. That first bear launched her bear-making business, Candy Bears, which Candy now runs from her new home in Seattle.

In addition to making teddy bears, Candy collects antique clothing. Many of her bears wear rompers or christening gowns that Candy copies from clothes in her collection. The careful hand-finishing of a bear's outfit often takes longer than making the bear itself.

Boy and *Girl* are 21 inches tall and jointed; they're made of mohair. He wears shorts, a shirt, and a bow; she wears a cotton dress and a ribbon ear bow.

Boy with Kite is 21 inches tall and jointed, with wooden knee joints; he is made of mohair, wears shorts, a shirt, and a bow, and carries a kite on a string.

Anne E. Cranshaw

Anne E. Cranshaw tells a bit of history with each of her teddy bears. Her grandfather Hammond Bradfield is remembered in two of Anne's bears, Hammond and Bradfield. John Rowe, who took part in the Boston Tea Party, is the "forebear" of another Cranshaw bear. John Rowe the teddy is dressed like an Indian—a disguise used by many of the colonists—but on his hip he carries a flask of nothing stronger than fine honey. Perhaps he plans to enjoy a cup of warm contraband tea and honey when he gets home.

Anne began making teddy bears after her then-five-year-old daughter, Joy, fell in love with the teddies the family had seen in a historic home during a house tour. Anne was thrilled by her child's reaction to the stuffed toys and realized then that teddy bears can make a real difference in a person's life. Today one of Anne's Bradfield bears keeps her elderly grandfather company, and other Cranshaw bears are used in a high-school counseling program to help students cope with hard times.

As much as Anne enjoys sharing her bears with other people, she gets even greater satisfaction from teaching classes in bear making. She says that watching someone finish her first bear is like watching a person fall in love for the first time. When the new bearmaker completes the last stitches on the face and sets the eyes, the teddy bear comes alive, and so does a special new sparkle in the bearmaker's heart.

Hammond is 18 inches tall and jointed; he is made of plush fabric and wears a satin bow.

John Rowe is 11½ inches tall and jointed; he is made of plush fabric, wears a colonial shirt and an Indian costume made of leather, glass beads, and feathers, and comes with a flask and a burlap-wrapped bale.

Many of Nancy Crowe's bears recall a year she spent in England as a student. Nancy says that during her year abroad she was usually traveling and people-watching, rather than studying. Her Muffin Man bear could have stepped off the streets of an English village. He carefully balances a tray of fresh bread and rolls on his head and wears the kind of waistcoat that a proper English muffin man would wear—no floury apron for him. Miss Emma Parkinson, Nancy's nanny bear, might have just come down from the nursery for tea; she's dressed in a real silk dress with a crisp apron that may even have a toy or two hidden in its pockets.

Nancy's bears are all fully jointed, classic teddy bears that she dresses in the finest silk and wool fabrics. Her Christmas bear is a lovely little white teddy dressed in an old-fashioned long coat. He looks very much like a Victorian Christmas card. The gentle look in his eye helps you remember snowy winter evenings with the family gathered around the fireplace.

Farnum T. Barnum could be the ringmaster of an American circus, but his European elegance is unmistakable. He is very much a gentlebear. Like all the bears that Nancy makes, Farnum is dignified yet cheerful. You might think of him as the leader of a troop of merry English entertainers on tour in the colonies.

Father Christmas is 13 inches tall and jointed; he is made of mohair, with Ultrasuede paws and glass eyes; wears a wool coat with a hood and alpaca lining; and carries a basket, miniature toys, and a staff.

The **Muffin Man** is 14 inches tall and jointed; he is made of mohair, with Ultrasuede paws and glass eyes; wears a wool jacket, waistcoat, cap, and scarf; and carries a tray of muffins and a brass bell.

Suzanne De Pee

Suzanne De Pee has worked with many crafts, but teddy bears are by far her favorite means of self-expression. Only teddies have character and innocence; they're always so much more than just pieces of fabric and wads of stuffing. Suzanne especially enjoys watching a teddy's face emerge. After she's completed a new bear, Suzanne carries on a long one-sided conversation with him. When he's heard all he needs to hear, she sends the bear on his way.

Suzanne's first bear was named Mousse; he has a cocked head and a mischievous nature. Since he wasn't able to sit still anyway, Suzanne bought him his own tricycle. When Buttercup came along, she wanted a tricycle just like her brother's, so Suzanne gave her one too.

As soon as Suzanne had put the last stitch in a new little gray bear, her youngest daughter, Heather, snatched it up and held on tight. Suzanne had to give up on ever getting her new bear back, so she made others from the same pattern and calls each of them Heather's Bear.

Suzanne's bear Tuffy had a sort of stern expression on his face when she first made him, but now he looks more gentle. Suzanne sensed Tuffy's loneliness and made him a companion, Buffy, with a strong, caring face and long arms to reach out and hug him. Both Tuffy and Buffy are content to sit side by side dreaming their own bear dreams.

Buffy and Tuffy.

*Clockwise from the top: **Tuffy, Buffy, Heather's Bear, Mousse, Buttercup,** and **Barnaby. Tuffy** and **Buffy** are 21 inches tall and jointed; they're made of mohair and have pigskin paws and glass eyes. **Heather's Bear** is 9 inches tall and jointed; she is made of alpaca fur, has pigskin paws and glass eyes, and wears a ribbon bow. **Mousse and Buttercup** are 8 inches tall and jointed; they are made of mohair, have pigskin paws and glass eyes, and wear bows. **Barnaby** is 13 inches tall and jointed; he is made of synthetic plush, has pigskin paws and glass eyes, and wears a ribbon.*

Suzanne De Pee

Mousse (left) and *Buttercup* (right) ride precision replicas of 1923 tricycles.

Heather's Bear.

Brenda Dewey

Brenda Dewey's first teddy bear, Amanda, disappeared when Brenda was eight years old, but she never forgot her long-lost friend. After her son Brian was born, Brenda wanted him to have a bear companion like Amanda. When she couldn't find a teddy bear that matched her treasured memory, Brenda decided to make a bear.

Brenda now has three children and her own bear-making business, Soda Fountain Bears. While she has continued to make traditional teddy bears like Brian's first bear, Brenda specializes in intricately dressed bears that might be characters in an elaborately staged production of a child's fantasy.

Humble Bumble is a backpacker bear that wanders through the woods with a tiny mouse, Jumble, in his pack. The mouse was Brian's idea. Because the little creature refuses to walk anywhere he can ride, Jumble is always in Humble's pack. They're constant companions, and neither is ever lonely.

Flutterbears are the product of Brenda's very special imagination. They're small, furry teddy bears that have been magically turned into fairies with gossamer wings and fluffy tutus. No two Flutterbears are exactly alike: Some are Fairies of the Seasons, others are fairies of the elements or butterflies. They recall children dressed for a ballet recital. Fairy of the Sea has her head ringed with pretend seaweed and real seashells. Her hand-dyed satin costume bounces over layers of net. Fire Fairy is dressed in red and orange; satin flames leap around her face. Air Fairy holds a tiny bird, and Earth Fairy is draped in spring flowers.

__Priscilla__ is 18 inches tall and jointed; she is made of Gumont mohair and wears an antique lace collar and a sterling-silver locket.

__Flutterbears__ are 9 inches tall and jointed; they are made of mohair and dressed in hand-dyed satin and netting with beads and flowers. These Flutterbears are the four __Fairies of the Seasons__.

Denise Dewire

Denise Dewire made her first teddy bear for her son. It was his Christmas present, and the boy and the bear became fast friends. But Denise's son wasn't the only one who was affected by that teddy bear; Denise found that making one bear led directly to making more teddy bears. She's made nearly 1,500 bears and has no plans to stop.

Denise's bear Yeoman 2nd Class is a traditional teddy bear. He's a copy of an old bear that has belonged to Denise for many years. Yeoman 1st Class has long been one of the favorites in Denise's collection of antique bears, so when she decided to make a replica of him, she wanted to give the bear the same sweet face and wise eyes. Like his ancestor, Yeoman 2nd Class wears a worn-out sailor suit and a dirty sailor's cap. When he's not out sailing his toy boat, Yeoman likes to play with his cousin Rebecca. They're about the same size, and she also looks like she might have belonged to a little girl growing up in the 1940s.

Denise designs all her own teddy bears. She makes many different kinds of bears, including one of her favorites, Bentley. He's an English school-boy bear that wears a hand-knitted sweater and a bow tie. Just one look at Bentley and you start thinking about setting a tea tray with buttered scones and jam tarts.

Bentley is 16 inches tall and jointed; he is made of German merino wool and wears a hand-knitted sweater, a cotton collar, and a bow tie.

Rebecca (left) is 12 inches tall and jointed; she is made of an English mohair blend, has glass eyes, and wears a cotton dress, panties, and bow. **Yeoman 2nd Class** (right) is 14 inches tall and jointed; he is made of German mohair, has glass eyes, and wears a cotton sailor suit and cap.

118

Sylvia Dombrowski

Jim and *Kate* are 22 inches tall and jointed; they are made of synthetic fur, wear blue and pink sailor outfits, and come with party balloons.

Sylvia Dombrowski isn't as nostalgic about teddy bears as some bearmakers are. Her bears aren't country folk, and they don't wear quaint Victorian costumes. The Barrister Bears are attorneys, nattily dressed in pin-striped vests and conservative ties. Each bear carries a scaled-down, monogrammed leather briefcase complete with briefs and legal pads.

Sylvia was a legal secretary for ten years, and most of her bears now make their homes with prominent attorneys. Sylvia has to chuckle when she tells about one lawyer—a partner in his firm—who said he wanted a Barrister Bear for his children but never got around to taking his bear home from the office. Other attorneys, including Sylvia's husband, think her bears are lucky and somehow help them to win more favorable decisions.

Sylvia has been making bears for only a few years, but they've quickly taken over her life. She even got married on Teddy Roosevelt's birthday. In honor of the day, Sylvia made a bear for each of her 140 wedding guests to take home. While she recognizes that the legal profession can use all the furry friends it can get, Sylvia also wants to make bears that aren't so stuffy. One of the great loves of her life is golf, so Sylvia is planning to make some fun-loving golfer bears. She also makes bears she calls the Toddlers; they're cubs dressed to match a child's favorite outfit.

Barrister Bears are 24 inches tall and jointed; they are made of synthetic fur, wear wool vests and silk ties, and come with leather briefcases.

Tatum Egelin

Tatum Egelin had never used a sewing machine until she began making teddy bears, but she has always loved old fabric. Tatum had collected boxes and boxes of synthetic furs, fine silks, and other fabrics. It seems as though all that material had just been waiting around for Tatum to make it into teddy bears. She made her first teddy bear for her grandson and found that she totally enjoyed working with fabric to make something that is bound to be loved.

One of Tatum's most-appealing teddies is dressed in a teddy. This bear is called Cindy Lou, and she reminds Tatum of a movie star from the 1940s. Cindy Lou is made of material that was used to make the fake-fur coats that were popular during World War II. The bear's lingerie is also made of vintage fabric.

Tatum likes to think that her bears preserve something of the past; she calls herself a salvage artist. Tatum found the wool felt for her bears' paws in the garage of a man who used to make poodle skirts in the 1950s and saved the scraps. She makes bears from bolts of alpaca and mohair that were originally intended for teddy-bear coats in the 1930s. Tatum doesn't like to overdress her bears; she likes the rich, old materials to be shown off to their best advantage. A sweater or a teddy is the most you'll find one of Tatum's bears wearing, and some teddy bears, like Cotton Candy, need no adornment to enhance their special fur coats.

Cotton Candy *is 17 inches tall and jointed; she is made of vintage fabric and wears a bow.*

Cindy Lou *is 17 inches tall and jointed; she is made of fabric from the 1940s and wears a silk teddy.*

Martha Fain

Martha Fain could never understand why grown-ups collected teddy bears until the day she happened to go into a teddy-bear shop. Before she knew what was happening, she was walking out of the store with her first Steiff bear tucked under her arm. Soon Martha was buying bears regularly, pretending that they were for her little son. Even though she told herself that someday the teddies would all be his, she kept them well out of harm's way on a high shelf. One thing led to another, and Martha found herself in a fabric store buying materials to make a teddy bear of her own.

Even though she says she was a flop at sewing when she took home economics, Martha soon got the hang of making teddy bears. She occasionally has to get a little help from her mother when her imagination exceeds the level of her skill, but most often Martha just lets her imagination and her needle go where they will. She may be inspired to start making a bear because she has seen a photograph of an antique teddy, but Martha never tries to copy the picture. She lets the bear take shape in her hands.

An old-time carousel inspired Martha to make Carousel Rabbit with a teddy riding its back. The memory of a production of *Swan Lake* inspired her elegant swan with a bear on his back steering him through the water with a wreath of flowers. Her bear Griz Kringle is the product of Martha's love for Victorian Santas and a celebration of her favorite season of the year.

Patsy is 10 inches tall and jointed; she is made of German synthetic fur and wears a lace collar with a bow.

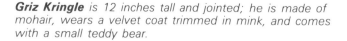

Griz Kringle is 12 inches tall and jointed; he is made of mohair, wears a velvet coat trimmed in mink, and comes with a small teddy bear.

Election Collection *is 12 inches tall and jointed; he is made of mohair, wears a glittery hat and a patriotic bow, and comes with an antique coin bank (not shown).*

Swan *is 15 inches long and made of merino wool;* ***Bear*** *is 9 inches tall and made of mohair. They come with a dried-flower wreath and the bear's crocheted hat.*

Carousel Rabbit *is 9 inches long;* ***Bear*** *is 4½ inches tall. They are made of merino wool and mohair, and come with a stand.*

Barbara Ferrier made her first teddy bear for her three-year-old son. The day she finished the bear, her son took his new friend along with him when he went to play at a neighbor's house. Before the boy came home for his nap, the neighbor had called Barbara to place an order for a teddy bear. Word of Barbara's teddy bears spread quickly through Nevada City, California, where Barbara lives, and she soon had orders for a dozen teddies. At this point Barbara decided she had to get serious about bear making. She developed her own designs and figured out how to meet her production goals. Over time her serious work has brought joy to people in all parts of the United States. She's so busy making bears and traveling to sell teddies that when her son wanted another bear recently he had to put in a written request.

Barbara tends to look at life with a glint of mischief in her eye, and she likes to make bears that have a sense of humor. She designed a bear named Eddie to look like her husband. The bear has knobby knees and elbows, and stands tall on legs that are especially skinny for a teddy bear. Barbara stuffs her bears Hope and Earnest in a special way that allows their floppy bodies to fit in close to the person who's hugging them. Cosmos, Roosevelt, and Snookie flaunt their enjoyment of life in a way that makes everyone smile.

Roosevelt is 11 inches tall and jointed; he is made of mohair and wears a ribbon with a wooden heart.

Earnest is 19 inches tall and jointed; he is made of distressed, hand-dyed mohair and wears a basic black bow.

Eddie is 9 inches tall and jointed; he is made of mohair and wears a wreath of artificial berries around his neck.

Cosmos is 6½ inches tall and jointed; he is made of hand-dyed alpaca and wears a ribbon around his neck. (The ribbon he comes with is not shown.)

Patricia Fici

Father Christmas is 12 inches tall and jointed; he is made of alpaca fur, has an angora mohair beard, and wears wool knitted undergarments, felt boots, and a wool overcoat and cap with mohair trim. He carries a pack full of Christmas surprises and wears a brass key on his belt.

Guinea pigs started Patricia Fici on her career as a bearmaker. When her two children were in preschool, they wanted to have guinea pigs at home just like the ones they had at school. Patricia was sure she didn't want to care for these pets, so she decided to make a pair of stuffed animals for her children. Giggles and Twiggles turned out to be very popular, easy-care substitutes for the real thing. Soon all the kids in the preschool were clamoring for Patricia's stuffed toys. In addition to guinea pigs, she made rabbits, brontosaurs, unicorns, and eventually teddy bears.

Patricia thinks of her bears as sculptures rather than toys. She hopes people will display her Father Christmas bear once a year and pass him on from generation to generation, so that the bear will become symbolic of the family's holiday feelings. He's a kindly old gentlebear with a glorious beard and an understanding look in his eyes. He has a key on his belt to unlock not only his workshop but all the Christmas spirit that is locked in everyone's heart. Patricia's bears Good Shepherd and Angelina could have just stepped off the makeshift stage of a school Christmas pageant.

In addition to her Christmas bears, Patricia makes a series of bears that represent the traditional roles of women. A busy homemaker is called Woman's Work Is Never Done. The Ladies of the Club are older and wiser than most of Patricia's bears. Each one peers serenely from under her mop cap and wraps her shawl tightly around her old shoulders.

The **Good Shepherd** is 12 inches tall and jointed. He is made of alpaca fur; wears silk and cotton robes, and leather sandals; and comes with a wooden crook and three handmade sheep.

Sandy Fleming

Sandy Fleming makes miniature bears that are so small and perfect that you want to button them in your pocket for safekeeping. She also makes bears that are so exquisitely dressed that you may feel they should be put in a cabinet alongside your fine porcelain dolls. In addition, Sandy makes cuddly teddy bears that you want to keep snuggled up against you or give to a child to hug.

Baby Cakes and Bunny Bear are less than two inches tall, but Sandy dresses them in tiny clothes. Baby Cakes wears a diaper and bunny slippers, and Bunny Bear wears pajamas. These bears may be tiny, but they are perfectly crafted teddies that are made entirely of Ultrasuede.

Annabelle is a towering 13½ inches. She is a confident little-girl bear that holds on tightly to a smaller teddy bear. Impeccably groomed and dressed, Annabelle not only wears a bonnet and carries a purse, but she's got on brand-new, white suede slippers. Jester Lee is also a well-dressed bear. A piece of wine-colored fabric inspired Sandy to make him. He may be beautifully costumed, with a silk ruff, but he wears his heart on his sleeve.

Woody, Blossom, Robert E. Lee, Reuben E. Lee, and Brambles are a different sort of bear. They've got pudgy tummies, perky noses, and bright, little eyes. They have a trusting, gentle look that lets you know they're eager to be your friend. Sandy's bears are everything that teddy bears should be. All you need to add is hugs.

Baby Cakes (left) is 1¾ inches tall and jointed; he is made of Ultrasuede and wears a diaper and removable bunny slippers. *Bunny Bear* (right) is 1¾ inches tall and jointed; she is made of Ultrasuede and wears a bunny sleeper with a removable hood.

Annabelle is 13½ inches tall and jointed; she's made of imported wavy wool. Annabelle wears a velvet dress, cotton pantaloons and petticoat, a lace collar, a wool hat, and Ultrasuede shoes, and a carries a crocheted purse and a small mohair teddy.

Etta Foran & Pat Joho

Teddy bears help us remember. They lead us back through time to the simpler days of our own childhoods and to shared memories of the past in which the smell of recently mowed lawns and home-baked bread are always predominant. Etta Foran and Pat Joho make Bearly Friends teddy bears that remind us of the folks in the town where we grew up or the town where we would like to have grown up.

Skeeter pumps his homemade scooter along the sidewalk, throwing newspapers neatly onto his customers' front steps. He works for the *Teddy News*, and you can be sure that all the news in the papers he throws is good news. Clyde could be any bear's little brother; he's the kind of cub that's lost half the time but always seems to make it home in time for supper. Bailey F.W. Bruin—the F. stands for Fred—is a roller-skating clown bear that travels with the circus. He's a small-town bear trying to make the big time, but at the end of the season, he may decide to pack up his bag of treasures and memories, and head for home.

Etta and Pat make bears in Joliet, Illinois. They come from different walks of life: Etta used to work in education, and Pat's career was medicine. They work on the bears together; neither has a specialty. Each woman does what needs to be done to give the individual bears their distinct personalities.

Clyde is 10 inches tall and jointed; he is made of synthetic plush that's sheared to different lengths and wears a cotton bow.

Skeeter is 15 inches tall and jointed; he is made of synthetic plush, wears a cotton cap, and comes with a news bag, rolled newspapers, and a wooden scooter.

Joyce Francies

Joyce Francies believes that teddy bears should have real work to do and their own stories to tell. You won't find any of her bears sitting around on quilts, staring into space. Clint is a sheriff bear intent on making his town safe for cubs and lady bears. Barnacle Bear is a wily pirate with buried treasure on his mind. McDonald the Miner pans for gold, and Sir Bearcelot eagerly defends fair maidens from dragons and other dangers. Joyce also makes grooms and brides, and bears that drive antique touring cars. When you look at one of Joyce's bears, you can almost hear him tell you his story.

Joyce lives in Placerville in California's gold country. Her great-grandfather McDonald was part of the gold rush of 1849. He never found gold; instead, he opened a general store that was also a stagecoach stop. McDonald's namesake bear has had more luck panning for gold. His rich golden fur may have given him a special advantage.

Barnacle Bear is a peg-legged tough guy; his trusted friend and constant companion is a parrot named Fred. Joyce attaches Fred to Barnacle's arm with velcro, so that when the pirate gets too rowdy, Fred can fly up to the top of a palm tree for safety until the bear calms down. Joyce is always amused when someone orders a Barnacle Bear with two furry feet and no peg leg; she sees having a wooden leg as an occupational hazard of pirating.

McDonald the Miner is 17 inches tall and jointed; he is made of acrylic fur and wears a homespun shirt, denim jeans, suspenders, and a felt hat. He comes with a tin prospector's pan.

Barnacle Bear is 17 inches tall and jointed; he is made of imported mohair fur, wears cotton clothes and a knitted watch cap, and comes with a wooden peg leg and a detachable parrot, which is made of acrylic fur.

Sir Bearcelot is 18 inches tall and jointed; he is made of imported mohair, wears pretend chain mail, and carries a wooden sword. **Puff the Musical Dragon** is made of acrylic plush and has a music box.

Clint is 18 inches tall and jointed; he is made of acrylic fur, wears a leather vest, a felt hat, and sheepskin chaps, and comes with his own sheriff's badge.

Gloria & Mike Franks

Gloria and Mike Franks live on a farm on Goose Creek in the hills of West Virginia, where they raise geese and peacocks, and make teddy bears. The couple is supposedly retired—she from her travel agency, he from the navy—but they've never been busier than they are now. They make about 500 bears each year.

Gloria has named many of their Goose Creek bears after friends or one of their five children. Her daughter-in-law Barri gave her name to Bearri Christmas. Timothy Lynn is named for their grown-up son; he's a chubby cub that has a sweet face and a look that's just a little sad, perhaps because he has recently left home to make his way in the wide world. A shy bear named Mickey can't quite raise his head to meet your eyes; he holds a bouquet of flowers behind his back. Mike Franks gives away a clue to this bear's human counterpart when he explains that Mickey may be bashful but he's a wonderful cook— just like the bearmaker himself. Whenever Gloria goes into town, she buys moire taffeta and soft silks to dress her girl bears. Abbear- Ionia shows off her first fancy party dress whenever she gets the chance. Other bears like Sonny and Sis wear sweaters that Gloria has knitted for them. But Worthington feels well dressed in just a simple plaid bow.

Worthington is 20 inches tall and jointed; he is made of acrylic and wears a bow.

Timothy Lynn is 15 inches tall and jointed; he is made of mohair, with mohair paws, and wears a ribbon bow.

Diane Gard

When Diane Gard was asked to write about herself for her twentieth high school reunion, she felt she had to embellish her life story. At the time Diane was not feeling especially successful in a conventional sense. She was an unemployed bookkeeper, an art major who wasn't working in art, and a single mother of two teenagers. But Diane had just completed her first teddy bear, so she decided to tell her former classmates that she ran a successful bear-making business. Her new career sounded so good on paper that Diane was inspired to start A Bear With A Heart, as she calls her company. By the time she actually went to the reunion, Diane had made and sold a dozen teddy bears. She could look anyone in the eye and say proudly that she was a professional bearmaker.

Diane has always loved old fabrics, and most of her teddy-bear designs begin when she finds a treasured fabric. Rough Rider got his start when Diane purchased cotton pile from a man who restored antique cars. The upholstery had been used for Pierce Arrow cars. Gray alpaca coats from World War II became her First Edition Bears. Theater seat covers and old carriage blankets have also become bears. Big Beau, Diane's largest and most flirtatious bear, is made from fine European mohair.

Each of Diane's bears has a little red heart on its chest. Diane says the hearts symbolize the love she brings to her work.

Third Edition Bear is 18 inches tall and jointed; he is made of vintage alpaca and has a ribbon around his neck.

Big Beau is 26 inches tall and jointed; he is made of imported mohair, wears a ribbon bow and his trademark glass heart, and holds a bunch of silk tulips behind his back.

144

Threadbear is 13 inches tall and jointed; he is made a horsehair carriage robe manufactured in the 1890s and comes with a red ribbon (not shown).

Rough Rider (left) and *Mrs. Rough Rider* (right) are 15 inches tall and jointed; they are made of cotton upholstery fabric. Over his heart he wears a commemorative medal made from ribbon and an Indian-head penny. She wears a muslin apron, with small ribbon flag over her heart, and carries a packet of love letters in her apron pocket.

Lori Gardiner

Lori Gardiner's teddy bears connect people with one another. She calls her teddy bears Echoes of the Past. Peggy Sue, her little bear in a felt poodle skirt, helps us remember the days of bobby socks and 45-r.p.m. records. Grandma and Grandpa are everyone's ideal grandparents. She is cuddly, plump, and loving; you could tell her anything and she would still love you. He is always ready to bounce a grandchild on his knee or pretend to pull out a quarter from behind a child's ear.

One of Lori's bears has a full-time job helping children in southern California. A social worker who works in an adoption program gives one of Lori's teddies to the child she is about to take to a new permanent home. She tells the scared child about all the other children the bear has helped her place in happy homes; somehow hugging that bear makes everything seem possible.

Making teddy bears is a family affair for Lori Gardiner. Her daughters, son-in-law, and even her granddaughter help her in the workshop. Whenever Lori finishes a bear and holds it up to be admired, one of her family members always says, "I think this is the cutest bear we've ever made." Everyone laughs; even though they've made hundreds of teddies, they can't help loving and admiring each one as he's about to go out into the world. The joy of shared work and love will stay with that teddy wherever he goes.

Peggy Sue is 16 inches tall and jointed; she is made of acrylic fur and wears a knitted sweater, a felt circular skirt, bobby socks, and saddle shoes.

Big Al is 14½ inches tall and jointed; he is made of acrylic plush, wears a tuxedo shirtfront, a bow tie, and top hat, and carries a cane.

Dolores & LeRoy Gould

Xion in two sizes: 11 and 13 inches. They are jointed and made of synthetic fur.

If you make teddy bears that are brown and cute, you're probably not very interested in what a real brown bear looks like. But Dolores and LeRoy Gould make pandas, and their pandas look a lot like real pandas. When the Goulds saw a real panda in the Nanjing Zoo in China, they were surprised by how much it resembled a very large animated toy. It was love at first sight for LeRoy, who arranged to go inside the panda's cage. He got within hugging distance of the animal he thinks is the most beautiful in the whole world. Lee should know; he and Dee have traveled the world from the Galapagos Islands to Australia to observe rare animals in their natural environment.

The Goulds try to make pandas that are as beautiful as the pandas in Nanjing. Their panda is jointed so that she can stand, scratch her ear, do a back bend, or lie on her back and hold on to her toe. Although they use the same pattern each time they make a panda, the Goulds have found that no two are exactly alike.

On a second trip to China, the Goulds photographed the only brown panda known to exist. To make their version of this awesome creature, the Goulds searched everywhere for exactly the right color of brown synthetic fur. They eventually located the color they needed and now make Xion (*Shee-on*), a beautiful remembrance of the rare brown panda.

Nanjing in three sizes: 8, 13, and 18 inches. They are jointed and made of synthetic fur.

Nancy Green

Nancy Green makes teeny tiny teddies that are perfect miniatures of classic full-size teddy bears. Nancy loves bears and has an extensive teddy-bear collection that was started by her husband. Whenever he came home from a business trip, he'd bring a bear with him. Before long teddy bears were also following Nancy home when she went shopping. The house was quickly overrun with bears, but that is precisely the way Nancy wants it. There was only one problem: Since the Greens liked teddy bears so much, they wanted to give bears to their friends and family; but once they bought a bear, they could never give it away. Nancy decided she would have to learn to make teddy bears for gifts, and she did.

A special bear Nancy calls her "treasure" inspired her to make her own tiny teddy bears. He's three inches tall and nearly perfect. Nancy's first tiny teddy is known as Elliott. He's named for Nancy's favorite college professor. Elliott is the sort of bear you can hide behind your calculus book and daydream about while the rest of the class works on equations. If you take home one of Nancy's Teddy Collection, the bear won't have a name, and its ribbon will be red. Nancy leaves the choice of a name and a pink or blue ribbon up to you. She says that if she gave her bears names and identities she would never be able to part with them.

Elliott *is 3 inches tall and jointed; he is made of nylon velvet and wears a bow.*

Teddy Collection *comes in three sizes: 2, 3, and 4 inches. They are made of nylon velvet and wear bows.*

Dolores Groseck

Dolores Groseck says that she made her first teddy bear to fill an empty chair. When she and her family moved to a new home, Dolores bought a large rocker for the living room. The chair just didn't look right to her, so she decided it needed to have a bear sitting in it. Dolores didn't just go out and buy a teddy; she signed up for a bear-making class. Her first teddy bear is still sitting in that big chair in her living room.

Dolores enjoys every aspect of making teddy bears, especially designing and sewing their clothes. She constantly draws on her training in art while she designs and produces bears. Her skill as a potter is evident in her bears' sculpted noses. Along with being carefully crafted, all of Dolores's bears have a quality she calls soul. Dolores says that while she doesn't expect you to talk to her bears, she insists that they talk to you.

Dolores finds inspiration for teddy bears in all kinds of odd and unusual places. Pagliacci developed out of a unique set of buttons and a friend's love for opera. Santa Bear is based on an old advertising picture of a child trying on an oversized Santa Claus costume. Fairy Catcher was to have been a fairy himself; but when Dolores saw Brenda Dewey's Flutterbears, she took her original idea a step further and made a magical bear with a net and mission to study fairies and then let them go.

Pagliacci is 22 inches tall and jointed; he is made of plush and wears a satin clown costume with old coat buttons.

Fairy Catcher is 22 inches tall and jointed; he is made of plush, has a clay nose, and is dressed in a homespun jacket and cotton stockings. He carries a fairy-catching net and comes with a clay fairy bear and a basket.

Santa Bear is 19 inches tall and jointed; he is made of plush and wears a fur coat and cap, with a small pillow tucked under his leather belt. He carries a burlap bag filled with wrapped packages.

Hope Hatch makes little bears with jointed knees that like to cavort in tiny spaces. One of Hope's first small bears lives happily in a briefcase. She made him for her brother who collects teddy bears and wanted to have a bear that was small enough to go along with him on business trips. Not all of Hope's teddies stow away in purses and briefcases: Some have been given to dolls and other bigger teddy bears to hold; others hang merrily on Christmas trees, enjoying a terrific view of all the festivities.

Hope started making teddy bears when her sister, who owns a fabric store, asked her to make a bear from a new pattern. Hope liked the bear but thought he was a little plain. She sees no reason for all teddy bears to be dull brown plush. Hope's bear Flash is gold lamé. Her Halloween bears are orange and black, and her Christmas bears are made from bright holiday fabrics. Other Hopefully Yours Bears are made from Ultrasuede and floral prints.

Each of the little bears that Hope makes is given a name. She feels that no two bears ever have the same personality, so their names reflect the diversity of character that can be found in three-inch teddies. Theo, Alice, Willow, Elisha, Adele, Sadie, and Ginger might all find their way out of Hope's workshop on the same day. They're all different, but each small bear is a little friend Hope has created to share.

Ginger is 3 inches tall and jointed; she is made of Ultrasuede and wears a ribbon bow with artificial flowers and a ribbon rosette.

Hope Hatch's bears cavort in the kitchen.

Frances Hayden

Maine winters are very cold, and in Damariscotta, Maine, where Frances Hayden lives, people bundle up in fur coats to keep warm. Generations of no-longer-stylish fur coats can be found in attics and thrift shops, so when Frances decided that she wanted to make real-fur teddy bears, she had no trouble finding materials.

Frances dreamed about making her first teddy bear before she made him. She had seen a bear-fur collar in an antique shop and dreamed about a real-fur teddy. She bought the fur piece and made the bear. When the owner of the antique shop saw the fur teddy, she wanted one made from a beaver skin that she'd had for a long time. Frances created a special bear for her. One teddy led to another, and now Frances makes wonderfully soft bears from all kinds of recycled fur. One of her teddies has even gone to live in Russia. An exchange student asked her to make a bear for him to take back home. The teddy is now in the Pioneer Camp in Artak, U.S.S.R.

A large black bear named Kyoto wears red Oriental pajamas. He's made of dyed seal fur, but most of Frances's teddy bears are made of beaver. Anitra is one of Frances's beaver bears; she wears a fancy ruff that sets off her rich fur to its best advantage. Occasionally someone asks Frances to make a teddy bear from an old mink stole. These bears are very special because they preserve so many memories.

Anitra is 22 inches tall and jointed; she is made of beaver fur and wears an antique lace collar with a satin ruffle.

Kyoto is 20 inches tall and jointed; he is made of seal fur and wears cotton pajamas.

Billee Henderson

Sometime during World War II, Billee Henderson's first beloved teddy bear got away from her. He was never found, and she still feels a little sad about her loss. She's made hundreds of delightful, classic jointed teddies; but they'll never make up for the old bear that got away.

While Billee was raising her five children, she sewed almost constantly, making clothes, drapes, and slipcovers. Now that her children have left home and she's a grandmother, Billee has time to use her sewing talents to make teddy bears. Her teddy Rufus is the color of a red fox. This boisterous little bear has a look in his eye that lets you know he'd rather be out climbing a tree than sitting quietly on a shelf. Billee also makes Pierrot bears and lady bears. Bierrot is dressed in white and black, with a sparkling tear falling from the corner of his eye. DuBeary is an elegant bear that Billee likes to pose with an old-fashioned parasol. This bear speaks softly and bats her eyelashes in the tradition of the best Southern belles.

When her busy schedule allows, Billee likes to make bears for charity. She is one of the Friends of BelAir Estates, a historic house in Bowie, Maryland, that is in need of extensive preservation work. Since this is horse country, Billee makes Teddy Arcaro, a jockey bear, to sell in the gift shop.

Rufus is 13 inches tall and jointed; he is made of mohair and wears a merino wool scarf.

DuBeary is 25 inches tall and jointed; she is made of mohair and wears a bow. The accessories shown are from the collection of the bearmaker.

There's more than just a little bit of country in each of Miriam Hertz's charming teddy bears. When they leave Miriam's attic workshop in her home in Oregon, Hertz Bears always carry something from the country with them. Sam takes his pet goose, Willy G., and Alexander brings along Bunny and a basketful of plump carrots in case his pet gets hungry.

Miriam believes that getting just the right expression on a bear's face is the most important part of her craft. She wants her teddies to look as though they're thinking nice thoughts. Miriam makes Hertz Bears in the classic way with jointed limbs, using fine mohair fabrics and careful handstitching. But she thinks of her bears as chubby children and sends them out into the world to bring joy to anyone who adopts them.

Miriam's teddy bear Sam is a farm boy. When he goes into town, he pulls his pet goose in a wagon. Country Cousin is also inseparable from his goose. He even takes his pet along when he goes to gather a basket of eggs. In addition to her folksy, country bears, Miriam also makes a charming little bear dressed in velvet that plays a perfectly crafted, tiny violin. You can imagine a proud bear family sitting around the parlor on Sunday afternoon listening to their talented cub play a Beethoven minuet.

Alexander is 15 inches tall; both he and *Bunny* are jointed and made of acrylic. Alexander wears wool pants, a collar, and a velvet bow tie, and carries a basket.

Country Cousin II is 15 inches tall and jointed; he is made of acrylic plush, wears wool pants with suspenders and a crocheted sweater, and carries a plush goose and a basket.

Sam is 15 inches tall and jointed; he is made of mohair and wears corduroy pants, a wool vest and matching cap, a collar, and a velvet bow tie. His pet goose, **Willy G.,** is acrylic and rides in his own wooden wagon.

Fritz is 14½ inches tall and jointed; he is made of mohair, wears wool shorts, a cotton shirt, and a velvet bow tie, and comes with a wooden violin and bow.

Dee Hockenberry

Dee Hockenberry says that she has often found herself making and selling bears just so that she can buy more antique teddies for her ever-growing collection. Dee began collecting teddies long before she made her first bear from a kit, but she soon realized that she wanted to make her own designs. Most of Dee's teddies are jesters or clowns, but there is something a little wistful about the expressions she gives her bears that allows them to reach out toward your heart.

While Dee was making her first Pagliacci bear, she noticed that the little fellow was looking particularly sad. She hadn't planned it, but Dee found herself sewing a tear on the bear's cheek. The clown's bright, ribbon-festooned costume and cap contrast sharply with his sad face. Elfabear is more cheerful; he's a Christmas sprite dressed in red and green. You can be sure he'll never be lonely because he carries a little bear called Elfie on his shoulder.

Dee calls her bear-making company Bears N Things. In addition to making about 300 teddies a year, Dee is a noted authority on collectible stuffed toys. She has written several books and often gives seminars on collecting old teddies. Her interest in the history of teddy bears is evident in Rose. She's an old-fashioned, traditional teddy bear with elongated arms and a humped back; but her poignant expression reflects Dee's kind heart.

Rose is 11 inches tall and jointed; she is made of dyed mohair and wears a lace ruff and ribbon.

Elfabear is 18 inches tall and jointed; he is made of mohair and wears a jester costume that's made of velvet, lamé, leather, and felt. *Elfie* is 6 inches tall and jointed; he's made of mohair.

Perry is 11 inches tall and jointed; he is made of mohair that's dyed to make his costume, which is completed with a ruff and a hat.

Pagliacci is 15 inches tall and jointed; he is made of distressed wool and alpaca that's dyed to make his costume, which is completed with ribbons, spangles, and a velvet hat.

171

Donna Hodges

Donna Hodges never has a problem thinking up a new teddy bear to make. She just thinks about her grandchildren, and pretty soon one of them suggests an idea for a bear. While she's sewing the teddy bear, Donna thinks about the child it will be named after, and a little of the child's personality seems to rub off on the teddy bear. Jessica, the prototype of Donna's newest bear, was completed the same day that her youngest grandchild was born. The bear wears a beautiful christening gown and smiles happily at you from her pram. Ashley has an ever-expanding wardrobe, just like a real teenager. Jodi Jester is named for Donna's oldest grandchild. The little bear is a clown, dressed in silk, lace, and lamé; this teddy seems to have a special quiet dignity.

Donna makes a series of six-and-one-half-inch bears that she calls Lil' Guys n' Gals; many of them are named for her grandchildren. There's Heather in a pink batiste dress, with her porcelain baby doll; Jeremiah in his favorite sailor suit and cap; Jake with his wooden train and an engineer's cap; Buddy Bear in overalls; and Apple Farm Bear, with a basket in her hand, about to pick a ripe apple.

Each of Donna's bears is childlike and innocent. Even the Papa Bear in her Three Bears set looks like he would be incapable of scaring Goldilocks. He looks so sweet and kind that he'd probably invite the little girl to come and live with the bear family.

Ashley is 14 inches tall and jointed; she is made of German mohair and wears a lace teddy. She comes with a wardrobe that contains her clothes and toys.

Jessica is 16 inches tall and jointed; she is made of llama, with Ultrasuede paws, and wears a batiste dress, slip, panties, and hat. Her pram is made of wicker and lined with fabric.

Jodi Jester *is 18 inches tall and jointed; he is made of mohair, wears a harlequin costume, and carries a puppet.*

Lil' Guys n' Gals *are 6½ inches tall and jointed; they are made of llama and silk, and come with clothes, accessories, and bases.*

Mary Holstad

Mary Holstad gives each of her teddy bears something to hold—a kitten, puppy, cheetah, lamb, bunny, or even a pig. When Mary was a child, she always seemed to be losing kittens. Her family would move to a new home and not bring along her kitty, or her little friend would somehow get lost. She's not sure now what happened to all her kittens, but the sense of loss has remained vivid in Mary's mind. She says that's why she gives her teddy bears pets of their own.

Katy's New Kitty was the first bear that Mary designed to hold a kitten. Katy clutches the kitten just as a child would, holding it tightly under the front legs and letting its body dangle. Held that way, the kitten looks almost as big as the teddy-bear child.

Mary is an artist who works primarily in pastels, drawing people and animals. Her teddy bears have the sense of a delicate drawing that has become three dimensional and may even be about to come to life. Her bears with pets, which Mary calls Best Friends, recall the special moment in a child's life when she is given a kitten. The young bear is both proud and tentative about her new pet, but under no circumstances would she want you to take the kitten away from her. If you did, she'd raise her down-turned paw over her eyes and pout until you returned her best friend.

My Best Friend.

My Best Friend *(left) and* ***Best Friends*** *(right) are 15 inches tall and jointed; both the bears and their kittens are made of mohair. The teddy on the left and in the picture above wears a cotton country-print dress with bloomers; the one on the right wears a Victorian-style dress with a lace bodice and pleated skirt.*

Nancy Howlan & Virginia Jasmer

Nancy Howlan and Virginia Jasmer make teddy bears together. They've been neighbors for many years, helping each other raise their families and finding time, when they could, to make quilts. Now that their children have grown up, Nancy and Virginia have embarked on a new career. They call their teddy-bear business Country Home Bears, although many of their bears are not, strictly speaking, country bears.

Myrtle and Maude are bears of means that have fallen on hard times in their old age. They dress in salvaged clothes and find joy in life's little pleasures, the first daffodil of spring or the first sparkle of frost on a window pane. While Myrtle and Maude are quietly dignified bears, Gidget and Wally are lively and giddy; they're 1950s bears on their way to a sock hop. She wears a pink poodle skirt and saddle oxfords; he's got on his favorite letter sweater. You can't help but smile at the innocence of these two hip teen bears.

After a hard day of bear making, Nancy and Virginia sit around the kitchen table, drinking tea and putting the final stitches on the last bears of the day. They talk about the bears that they have made and the bears they plan to make. Sometimes a bear will remind them of someone they've known, but usually they like to think about what the teddy bear's life will be like in the place to which they will ship him after he's completed.

Myrtle and *Maude* are 20 inches tall and jointed; they are made of acrylic fur and carry bags made from drapery fabric. They wear fur coats; old hats decorated with flowers, feathers, and beads; tattered stockings; and hiking boots.

Gidget and *Wally* are 20 inches tall and jointed; they're made of acrylic fur. She wears a felt skirt, sweater, bobby socks, and saddle shoes. He wears jeans and a letter sweater.

Hillary Hulen & David Reugg

Cleveland is 20 inches tall and fully jointed; he is made of English alpaca, has a growler, and wears a satin patriotic hat and ribbons.

Hillary Hulen and David Ruegg did not have teddy bears on their minds the day they first met. They were both intent on finding a rare woodpecker in a national park in Texas. Neither Hillary nor David ever sighted the bird, but they found each other. They now live in Oregon in a farmhouse where they make Heidibears.

Hillary says that she made her first teddy bear because she was cold. One fall David kept putting off cleaning out their wood stove, so they couldn't safely have a fire. Hillary, who was home all day, got very cold. She fell asleep and dreamed of a warm little bear. When she woke up, Hillary decided to make Muffy—a cuddly bear with her paws tucked in a little bear muff. The bear also wears a hat and scarf to keep her warm. As soon as David saw the beautiful, bundled-up bear, he cleaned the stove, lit a fire, and started encouraging Hillary to keep making bears.

One of Hillary's bears is called Opal; she is a keeper of memories and wears a heart-shaped container of potpourri around her neck. Hillary makes the potpourri herself from a batch that her grandmother started with the dried roses from her wedding bouquet. Hillary often adds dried flowers from bouquets that have been special to her to the sweet-smelling mixture. Another Heidibear is called Harry Truman. He's a little bear that looks you straight in the eye as if to say, "The buck stops here." Cleveland isn't quite so serious; he's got a bit of fun in his eyes.

Muffy is 12 inches tall and fully jointed; she is made of alpaca, wears a wool scarf, and carries an alpaca muff.

After the lights are out at night and everyone is asleep, teddy bears and toys come alive and move about the house. Remember when you believed this? Ann Inman remembers and makes teddies that actually move. Ginny and Nicholas are cubs that cuddle smaller teddy bears and hold glowing candles that will light their way up the stairs to bed. Merlin lifts a glimmering crystal ball. He moves his head from side to side as though he was deep in thought about the images of the future he has seen in his magic sphere.

Ann doesn't always make teddy bears that move, but her mechanical bears are her favorites. After she first got the idea that she would like to make bears that seemed to be alive because they could move, Ann spent a long time searching for someone who had the mechanical skills to animate her bears. She finally found someone who could make her bears move in exactly the way she wanted them to. The bears are powered by electric motors, and each not only moves but also holds a light. Many of Ann's bears have found their way into store windows where they bring a bit of their magic to everyone who passes by.

Ann is hoping to interject even more magic and motion in the teddy bears she makes. She is currently working on a ballerina bear that will dance and a jack-in-the-box that will pop up.

Merlin is 26 inches tall, not counting his hat; he's made on a custom-built steel frame with merino wool. His cloak and hat are velvet and lamé, and he comes with an internally lit "crystal" ball.

Lady Bear is 11 inches tall and jointed; she is made of dyed mohair and wears a lace skirt and pearls.

Trudy Jacobson

Trudy Jacobson grew up in a small town in southeastern Kansas. Her grandfather lived on a farm just outside town, and Trudy often stayed with him and helped out with farm chores. Her teddy bears have a genuine country feeling about them. They look clean, poor, and proud like long-forgotten relatives pictured in an old family album.

Bethel wears a homemade cotton dress and carries her pet rabbit tightly clasped in her arms. A look of age and country wisdom shows in her face even though she is just a young bear. Artie McKinley is a tough character. He's a plaid teddy bear without so much as a bow to soften his hard look. Old-Time Teddy is just an old softy. Unlike his best friend, Artie, this bear seems to be asking you to pour out your troubles to him. Even Trudy's peddler, Lenah Nelva, is a country bear, rather than a sophisticated merchant from the city. She wears a print dress and has an understanding look about her face. Lenah Nelva could be a farm woman taking her jams and homemade butter to the city to sell.

Teddy Bears by Trudy pull at your heartstrings and remind you of your simple country roots. Her teddy bears have the kind of basic strength of character that you often see etched in the faces of country folk by wind, rain, and their hard lives.

Lenah Nelva is 15 inches tall; she is made of wool fabric and has wooden joints. The peddler is dressed in a cotton pinafore and cloak, and carries baskets that are made in Missouri and a **Butterscotch Baby** bear.

Bethel and her Bunny (left) are made of plush. She is 17 inches tall, jointed, and wears a cotton dress, pinafore, and bonnet. *Melody's Baby* (right) is 8½ inches tall and jointed; he is made of plush and wears a diaper and a bonnet.

Jerry & Morgan Jurdan

Jerry and Morgan Jurdan live in an enchanted forest in the shadow of Mount St. Helens. Together they make Wizard Bears and Shaman Bears. Living in the forest and knowing firsthand the power and majesty of the Earth, the Jurdans have learned to recognize the special connection between all living things on the planet. They hope that the teddy bears they make will help people feel as they do about the preciousness of all life.

Attention to detail is a hallmark of J & M Uniques. The company began when Jerry was laid off from his job, and a hobby suddenly had to be turned into a money-making occupation. From the beginning, Jerry and Morgan have paid as much attention to the accessories that they make for their bears as to the detailing of teddies themselves. Some Wizard Bears come with desks that are hand-built from fine hardwood. No two desks are ever exactly alike; some are simple and others intricate, but they all contain bottles of potions and the other ingredients needed for the Wizard's magic. The Shaman Bear has pouches of crystals and magic gear, and a special staff. Moxxie Fisherman carries a fishing rod that actually works.

While most of the Jurdan's bears seem to be at home in an enchanted forest, the Entertainer is pure Hollywood. He comes with a top hat and cane, and his own stool where he can sit when he delivers one-liners between song-and-dance numbers.

The **Entertainer** is 17 inches tall and fully jointed; he is made of West German plush, wears a top hat, a vest, and a satin bow, and comes with a stool and a cane with a brass top.

Moxxie Fisherman is 13 inches tall and jointed; he is made of imported mohair, wears a fishing vest and straw hat, and comes with a working fishing pole and an assortment of tied flies.

Wizard Bear is 14 inches tall and jointed; he is made of plush and wears a cape made of many fabrics. He comes with a velour dragon and a handbuilt stool and desk, which is stocked with the tools of his trade.

Shaman Bear is 17 inches tall and jointed; she is made of West German plush and has a leather nose. She is dressed in a cape made of fabric, leather, Ultrasuede, feathers, glass and metal beads, and bells. She carries a staff topped with fabric and crystals, and wears leather pouches filled with relics, cures, and herbs.

Charlotte Kane

Charlotte Kane often walks along the beach near her home in Massachusetts. While she's out walking, she collects small smooth rocks called popplestones. Charlotte also makes up tales about a colony of bears that migrated to the shore of the Atlantic Ocean from their original home in northern Canada. The bears settled on an isolated strip of beach, finding that the more-moderate climate suited them better than the bitter cold of the far north. One of the cubs that was especially fond of playing in the waves and walking along the shore first discovered popplestones. He began carrying one of the little round rocks in a pouch on a cord around his neck. The cub believed that the popplestone was magic and brought him just enough good luck to make a difference in his life, just enough to make everything go a little bit smoother. Since none of the other bears could prove that the stone was not magic, they all began to carry popplestones.

Charlotte calls her teddy bears Popplestone Bears. The designs for the bears are created by Carole Bowling, a dollmaker, but Charlotte's craft brings the teddies to life and gives them their special smiles.

One of Charlotte's most endearing bears, Ginger-Peachy, is an adaptable little fellow: In one position he looks ever so serious; in another his bright smile is pure joy. He likes to sit with his arms behind his back and face the world with a big grin.

Ginger-Peachy (two shown) is 11 inches tall and unjointed; he is made of plush fabric and wears a satin bow.

Poppy is 18 inches tall and wired; he or she is made of German plush. The adult bear comes with a cub, *Li'l Pops*, in a leather backpack. The cub is 8 inches tall, made of plush, and carries a cloth doll named *Ali-oop,* which is made by Carole Bowling.

Doris King makes teddy bears that speak through their eyes directly to your heart. The bear that she calls Bearly Makin' It has a mournful look on his face that belies his perky bunny slippers. He looks as though he's had the flu for several days and just doesn't seem to be getting any better. This little bear is exactly what the doctor ordered for a sick friend who needs a sympathetic teddy bear to cuddle up with for an extended period of bed rest.

Doris made her first teddy because her daughter bought her a book on bear making and insisted that she make one. She soon threw out the book and started making teddy bears that look old even though they're brand-new. Doris says that her bears are "preloved." Doris's teddies George, Prissy, and Foxy Lady are old-fashioned bears made of distressed mohair. Prissy likes to wear an old hat or just a faded silk flower; George is a gentlebear that offers you a ready paw for holding and has a face that says, "I care."

Not all of Doris's bears are serious teddies that seem eager to sit down and listen to your problems. The bear Davin is young and carefree. His namesake is Doris's grandson, and both the boy and the bear are mischievous tree climbers. Davin keeps the pockets of his jeans stuffed with all the necessities of a cub's or a boy's life: a slingshot, a comb, a bag of marbles, a hook on a string, and a slimy worm.

Davin is 13 inches tall and jointed; he is made of alpaca and wears worn-out blue jeans, a cotton shirt, and a baseball cap.

Bearly Makin' It (left) is 13 inches tall and jointed; he is made of acrylic fur, wraps up in a patchwork quilt, and wears felt bunny slippers. *Doctor Bear* (right) is 13 inches tall and jointed; he is made of acrylic fur and wears a surgical gown, with cap, mask, and shoe covers.

Foxy Lady is 18 inches tall and jointed; she's made of distressed mohair.

Prissy is 15 inches tall and jointed; she is made of distressed mohair and wears an old hat.

George is 19 inches tall and jointed; he is made of distressed mohair and wears an old shirt collar.

Sue Kruse

When Sue Kruse makes up a new teddy bear, she names it and gives it a life story, plenty of relatives and friends, and a few important ancestors. That bear is hers to keep, but the teddies that she makes from its pattern will have to find other homes, so Sue tries very hard not to become attached to them. She doesn't even give them names; she leaves that up to the people her teddy bears will live with.

Sue's largest bear is Captain Cornelius. He's 24 inches tall and looks very much like a Steiff bear. Cornelius's face looks worn and tired; he's obviously traveled far and seen much. Beresford also looks as through he's been around for a long time. Sue ages the fabric with which she makes both of these bears with a special process that took her two years of experimenting to develop. But the result of Sue's hard work is a teddy bear that looks like its been loved dearly by at least one child. One of Sue's bears was actually mistaken for an old Steiff teddy bear.

An old rag doll inspired Sue to make her bear Mabel. The doll was so worn that she had obviously been very well loved, and Sue wanted to make a bear that would convey the tired-out but loving feeling of the rag doll. Her washtub full of clothes and the caring look on her face make it clear that this bear's work is never done: She'll always be taking care of you.

Captain Cornelius is 24 inches tall and jointed; he is made of distressed synthetic fur and wears a child's sailor shirt.

Mabel is 12 inches tall and jointed; she is made of synthetic fur and wears a cotton-print dress and underskirt, a sugar-sack apron, and a bandanna. She comes with a washtub and a washboard.

Jacque Kudner

Jacque Kudner has found a way to combine her two favorite occupations—collecting antiques and making bears. She makes teddy bears that incorporate antique buttons or other memorabilia. Her bear Timely has an antique pocket watch tucked in a special pocket on his belly, and Hoppi, a bear that is dressed like an old-fashioned bellhop, carries an antique brass key.

Jacque makes classic teddy bears and has often been inspired to make a bear by a picture in an old book. Her Three Bears seem to have stepped off the pages of a Victorian storybook about a family of well-dressed, urban bears. You can imagine PaPa Bear pulling on his tailored topcoat and calling to MaMa Bear and Baby Bear to join him for a walk around the park. If Goldilocks wanders in while they are out, she is likely to find a well-appointed house with gaslights and steam heating.

The first Jacquebear was a present Jacque made for her first child soon after he was born. Jacque felt confident that she could make a teddy bear that was superior to any of the store-bought bears in her son's growing collection. Jacque had been sewing her own clothes since she was a teenager. She has a bachelor's degree in fine arts with an emphasis on textiles and a master's degree in fibers. Jacque knew she could make a good teddy bear and she did. Jacquebears are gentle, fun-loving bears that are made even more special because of Jacque's love for antiques.

The **Three Bears** are jointed; they are made of mohair and wear woolen, linen, and silk clothes. **PaPa** is 15 inches tall, **MaMa** is 14 inches tall, and **Baby** is 10 inches tall.

Hoppi is 15 inches tall and jointed; he is made of mohair and wears a satin jacket and hat.

Sharon Lapointe

Sharon Lapointe believes that if you can imagine teddy bears as gold miners and ballerinas, you can really let your imagination go wild and envision merbears, those fascinating sea creatures that have often enchanted salty sailor bears when they sailed through uncharted seas. Sharon's merbears, Emerald and Opal, are 30 inches long from the tops of their furry ears to the bottoms of their glimmering fish tails. They are as rare as mermaids because Sharon doesn't make very many, since she has to be in a very special mood to tackle the difficult process of crafting a merbear.

Designing and manufacturing Enchanted Bears is a full-time occupation for Sharon. She is always thinking about teddy bears or making teddy bears. To help her children and their friends understand what she does all day, Sharon has made it her practice to visit her children's kindergarten classrooms. She takes along finished bears, patterns, and teddy-bear parts, and shows the children how teddies are made.

The first teddy bear to find its way into Sharon's heart now sits in semiretirement on a shelf in her house. The teddy originally belonged to Sharon's father, but she and her brothers, sisters, and cousins played with him whenever they went to visit their grandmother. Even her own children played with the well-loved teddy. Now he sits in relative peace; his main purpose is to inspire Sharon to make honest, hard-loving teddy bears as well as her more fanciful bears.

Buttercup *is 15 inches tall and jointed; he is made of mohair, with leather paws, and wears a ribbon bow.*

Emerald *(left) and* ***Opal*** *(right) are 30 inches tall and jointed; they are made of mohair and metallic fabric, and wear scallop shells and artificial flowers.*

Mary Kaye Lee

Here goes **Harvey** off into the wild blue yonder.

Mary Kaye Lee fell in love with Steiff teddy bears when she was a little girl pressing her nose against the window of the neighborhood toy store. While she was in high school, Mary Kaye saved her money and started buying teddy bears. Her bear collection has grown to more than 700 teddies, not including the bears she has made herself.

Before she became a bearmaker, Mary Kaye designed and sold quilts. Her quilts were on the cover of *Better Homes and Gardens*; and her store, Quilts in the Attic, was very successful. But after her husband's death, Mary Kaye found that she really needed to get back to her teddy bears. At first she sewed for teddies, making pinafores and shirts. As Mary Kaye watched people trying her clothes on their bears, she began to imagine a very special teddy called Harvey, Mary Kaye's first and best-loved bear.

Harvey has traveled the world with Mary Kaye. They've shared adventures in the Bahamas, Brazil, France, Spain, Switzerland, Japan, and Nepal. Mary Kaye chronicles Harvey's trip to the Grand Canyon in a limited-edition book. Harvey is an especially charming bear that smiles at the world and usually finds his smile returned. Mary Kaye also makes Bear Lee, a sweet little bear with a Swiss music box that plays "Teddy Bears' Picnic." Chris the Paperboy is named after Mary Kaye's son. When she introduced him to his namesake, her grown-up son laughed and cooed, "Oh, I had such a furry little face."

Harvey is 16 inches tall and fully jointed; he is made of alpaca and wears a leather vest and a brass Colorado marshal's badge.

Chris the Paperboy is 13 inches tall and jointed; he is made of West German mohair, wears a cap, and carries a leather bag with reduced copies of The Denver Post.

Bear Lee is 22 inches tall and jointed; she is made of mohair and has a Swiss music box that plays "Teddy Bears' Picnic."

Althea Leistikow

Althea Leistikow is a bearmaker who has an artist's imagination. If she can picture something in her mind, Althea can pick up scissors and cloth, and transform her mental image into reality. Before she begins making a new teddy bear, Althea wants to know the bear's name, the story of his life, and the character and identity of his ancestors. Once she has shaped a bear in her imagination, it's only a matter of time until he's sitting on a shelf waiting to be hugged.

The Old Timer began with a memory of a childhood vacation in Yellowstone National Park. As the image of this bear formed in Althea's mind, she remembered both the real bears that came up to the car windows begging for food and also Old Scarface, the teddy bear that accompanied her on the trip. Althea makes the Old Timer with worn-out paws and a slightly scruffy look.

Teddiwog's Three Ring Circus is a bear-making extravaganza of fabrics, fur, and feathers. Sir Tiny Teddy proudly rides his trained seal, Super Seal. Miss Goldie T. Teddy wears a gold-lamé cape and feathers as she guides Li'l Eli, her elephant, into the ring.

Christmas has always been a special time in Althea's family, and each year she adds to the celebration by creating a new Belsnickle. This little Santa Claus comes from the holiday traditions of German immigrants to the United States. He is said to bring evergreen boughs, good things to eat, presents, and if necessary, switches to families.

Miss Goldie T. Teddy *and **Li'l Eli** together are 16 inches tall. She is made of pile and dressed in lame, with a feather headdress; the elephant is made of a nubby-pile fabric.*

Teddy Goldenwood *is 16 inches tall and jointed; he is made of mohair and wears a ribbon or a Pendleton scarf (not shown).*

Lynn Lumley

Teddy bears have been a lifeline for Lynn Lumley. When Lynn started making tiny teddies, she was out of work and living in a town where she didn't know anybody. Lynn tried to make ends meet by selling the crafts she made, but she just couldn't seem to manage. Then one day she created a teddy bear. Lynn filled his little face with loving care, and with true teddy-bear generosity, that first teddy and all his little brothers and sisters have taken good care of Lynn. She's now a successful bearmaker, who can't seem to make enough teddies to keep up with the requests she receives.

Lynn's Doorstep Teddy is a tiny bear wrapped in a patchwork quilt and placed in a basket. He's an orphan bear, waiting for a kind person to adopt him. Doorstep Teddy is a sad, little creature, but Cecilia and Eddie are full of joy and hope. They are Lynn's wedding-couple bears. Eddie looks like he's just about to burst with love and pride, while Cecilia seems to be more innocent and shy. Cecilia has been dressed by her loving grandmother; every rose in her headpiece is handmade by Lynn.

The Jester bear that Lynn makes is all smiles and laughter. If he is shy, he hides his timidity behind a happy mask. He's the kind of bear you could call on to help you get through a difficult situation. And that, as Lynn says, is what teddy bears are all about.

Andy (both sizes shown) is 5½ or 6½ inches tall and jointed; he is made of llama and wears a bow.

Mary Ellen is 5½ inches tall and jointed; she is made of llama, wears a cotton dress decorated with fancy work, a straw hat, socks, and patent-leather shoes, and carries a basket and a Kewpie doll.

Jeanie Major

Making teddy bears is a hobby for Jeanie Major; but she's always working on a bear when she's not taking care of home, kids, and puppies, or doing volunteer work. Jeanie has loved teddies since she was a small child. In almost every family photo from Jeanie's childhood, she has a bear under each arm. Her mother made her first teddy bear from flannel scraps left over from pajamas. Now Jeanie's own children romp through the woods around her home near Puget Sound, clutching teddy bears their mom has made.

Jeanie has created many kinds of bears; each one has a personal significance for her. The Pacific Northwest Berry Bears are dyed to match the colors of the berries that grow near the Major's home: blueberries, huckleberries, strawberries, boysenberries, and salmonberries. The Berry Bears have smiles as sweet as the ripe berries they're named for. To commemorate her husband's service in Vietnam, Jeanie made the 'Nam Bear. When she teaches her Sunday school class, Jeanie takes along a teddy dressed to illustrate a Bible story. One week he plays the part of baby Moses, wrapped in a diaper lying in a basket; another week, he's Joseph in his coat of many colors.

One of Jeanie's most unusual bears is Country Andy. He's part bear and part Raggedy Andy doll. Jeanie says that she always felt her rag doll wanted to be a teddy bear. When she makes a Country Andy, Jeanie feels that she's giving her old rag doll his heartfelt wish.

Country Andy is 16 inches tall and jointed; he is made of German mohair, with yarn hair and cotton-fabric legs, and wears a cotton romper.

Pacific Northwest Berry Bears are 11 inches tall and jointed; they are made of distressed mohair that's dyed berry colors and have lace colors around their necks and artificial berry chaplets.

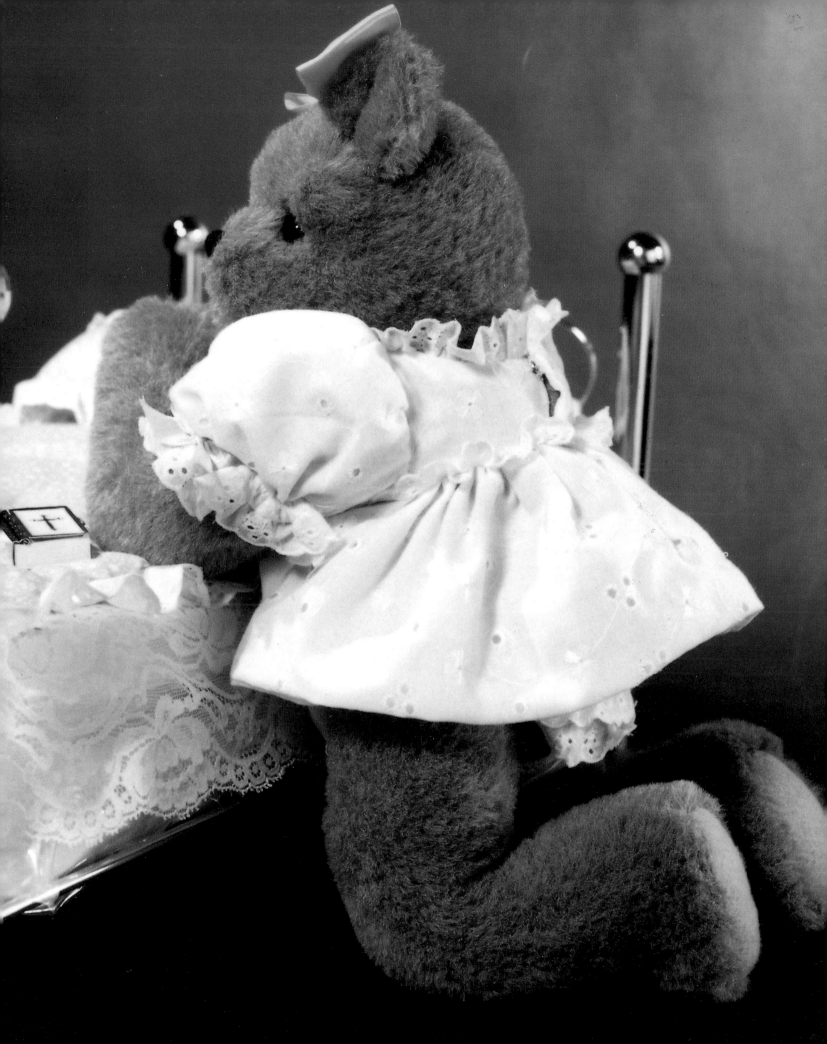

Chuck & Judy Malinski

Judy Malinski made her first teddy bear from a scrap of synthetic fur left over from a sofa pillow. She says that most of her first teddies looked more like chimpanzees than bears and that her relatives dreaded receiving them as gifts. If this is true, Judy has advanced considerably in her bear-making skills because anyone would be thrilled to find a bear like Quint or Lorraine under the Christmas tree.

Quint is a charismatic little teddy that can hold any pose. He especially enjoys headstands, back bends, and an occasional push-up. Quint is one of the first teddy bears for which Chuck and Judy perfected a pattern. Lorraine is a much more serious bear than Quint. Her knees are bent, her hands folded, and her head is bowed in prayer. You can almost hear her saying, "Now I lay me down to sleep." If you touch her right paw, she plays Brahms's Lullaby.

When Chuck joined Judy at the sewing table, Judy K. M. Bears became a full-time business. For the first two years, they worked on their porch in Anaheim, California. Brownie troops, Head Start classes, and lost tourists came by to see what was going on and stayed to have a soda, hold a bear, and hear a story. After their bear-making business was firmly established, Chuck and Judy closed their shop and went on the road. They now travel about 75,000 miles a year, making teddy bears as they go.

Ben is 13½ inches tall and jointed; he is made of alpaca and wears a hand-knitted vest.

Lorraine is 13½ inches tall (kneeling) and jointed; she is made of alpaca, has an electronic music box, and wears a short nightgown with matching panties.

Cleo Marshall

Cleo Marshall learned to sew before she even started school. Her grandmother taught her, and together they spent many happy hours making doll clothes and quilting. As an adult Cleo confined her needlework to making children's clothes and mending wear and tear, until an illness caused her to be housebound for a few years. To keep herself busy and lift her spirits, Cleo began making teddy bears.

Cleo makes three sizes of bears—all less than four inches tall. Her teddies are made entirely by hand. Big Daddy measures three and three-quarters inches. He's a gentle bear that wants to take care of everything and always has a shoulder ready for you to lean on. Mama is shorter and just a little plump. Like most mothers, she has more to do than she can ever hope to accomplish, so she looks slightly harried.

Baby is Cleo's favorite teddy bear. He's two and one-half inches tall, and Cleo never knows whether a new Baby will be a boy or girl until the little bear is completed. Looking at pictures of real baby bears, Cleo was struck by how much their proportions are the same as human babies. The cubs' heads are large, they have big eyes and ears, and their bodies are short and round. She also noticed that every cub had a slightly different expression on his face in much the same way that the faces of human babies show the beginnings of their unique personalities. Cleo's Baby bears are all cuddly cubs, but no two look exactly alike.

Baby is 2½ inches tall and jointed; she is made of velvet upholstery fabric.

Big Daddy is 3¾ inches tall, **Mama** is 3¼ inches tall, and **Baby** is 2½ inches tall. They are jointed and made of velvet upholstery fabric.

Carol Martin

After many years of faithful service, Carol Martin retired her childhood teddy bear to the attic. He sat quietly in a dusty corner while Carol married and took off for the adventures of her new life. The bear waited patiently, and finally one day Carol climbed the stairs to the attic and retrieved her old friend. This worn-out teddy now has a new career inspiring Carol to design and make teddy bears.

The first bear Carol made was three feet tall. The project was so difficult that she swore she would never make another bear. Before long the memory of an old photograph of her sister Alice Mae started Carol making a toddler bear, dressed in pink. The little bear carries a pink purse with a 1943 steel penny tucked inside. The penny was minted the year Carol's sister was born.

Carol also makes bears that she names after her father and her mother. Mr. French is a lovable papa bear that spent his first months in the hospital helping Carol's dad recover from a serious illness. Mr. French the teddy bear has an exceptionally long nose; and some people erroneously believe that Mr. French the person shares the same trait. He doesn't. Carol has learned that if you name teddy bears after your relatives, people are going to make comparisons that are not always favorable to the bears or the humans.

Mr. French is 15 inches tall and jointed; he is made of mohair, with leather paws and glass eyes, and wears a collar and necktie.

Opal is 12 inches tall and jointed; she is made of mohair, wears a bow, and comes with knitting needles, yarn, and a hassock.

Bonnie Waas McCabe

Bonnie Waas McCabe has been making and selling her craftwork since she was eight years old, but she'd rather make teddy bears than anything else. Bonnie didn't feel this way about bears when she was making her first teddy. She wasn't even sure that she would ever finish that bear. Bonnie made the bear from a pattern that she found in a library book, and the teddy bear took her three weeks to complete. Bonnie thought that she would never make another bear, but before long the teddy had a husband and a cub, and now she's the grandmother of hundreds of teddy bears.

Bonnie's bears are uniquely appealing. Her bear Rags is the antithesis of well-groomed bears with carefully brushed fur and crisp bows. His fur is messy and his bow is scruffy, but Rags is irresistible. Tail-er Bee Honey has a perplexed expression on his face. A bee has landed on his tail, and he is unsure what he should do. Gullibear Trabels is a stowaway bear that loves to travel but can't afford airfare.

Bonnie says that her teddy bears choose whether they will be boy or girl bears while she's making them. She once had a rush order for a fancy-dressed bear, but the bear she was making wouldn't conform to her design for a very feminine teddy. No matter how much she worked on the bear he insisted that he was not going to wear frilly clothes. Bonnie finally gave up and made a new bear; this one was a girl, and she was thrilled with her fancy clothes.

Rags is 15 inches tall and jointed; he is made of acrylic fur and wears a cotton bow.

Pierrot Bears are 15 inches tall and jointed; they are made of acrylic and cotton fur, and wear satin hats and collars.

Maureen McElwain

Rhonda is 18 inches tall and jointed; she is made of synthetic fur, wears flowers on her head, and carries a basket of flowers.

To some people, making teddy bears might seem the last thing that Maureen McElwain needed to include in her busy life. She's a banker, a mother of teenagers, and an avid clogger who teaches folk dancing two nights a week. But when a friend insisted that Maureen would really enjoy making bears, she went right out and bought all the materials needed to construct a teddy. Two days later Maureen finished her first bear and started on her second.

Maureen's father got her started repairing old teddy bears. He showed one of Maureen's bears to a friend. The teddy got the man thinking about his 85-year-old bear that was in very bad shape; he asked Maureen if she could repair it. Maureen worked carefully to put the old teddy back together, and when he was ready to go back home, she and her children took him out to dinner. Maureen's bear Cy is a copy of the old bear; she says that he is worn but wise.

The Banker Bear is Maureen's first character bear. He has a way of looking both pleasant and stern at the same time. Mrs. B is Banker Bear's wife; she has a weakness for fancy clothes, which her husband happily indulges. Maureen's bear Sue actually works at the bank. She is a Desk Bear and puts in long hours on a corner of Maureen's desk, watching and listening to all that goes on during the hectic workday.

Mrs. B (left) is 18 inches tall and jointed; she is made of synthetic fur and wears a crocheted collar and a mink stole. **Banker Bear** (right) is 18 inches tall and jointed; he is made of synthetic fur, with suede paws, and wears a vest, a tie with tie tack, and a watch chain.

Flora Mediate

The first bear that Flora Mediate made has a dark-brown body and a light-brown muzzle. Flora has made many other bears since she made him, but this bear has always been her favorite. She never understood exactly why she liked that particular bear so much until she found a picture of herself as a child. In the photograph she is holding her teddy bear, and he is also dark brown with a lighter muzzle.

Flora makes many bears that wear elaborate outfits, but her teddy Mac Kendree is a plain bear that wears nothing but a bow and a smile. He's a traditional teddy, so Flora named him after her grandfather, who didn't exactly appreciate the modern world. Uncle Sam is anything but a plain teddy bear. He wears red, white, and blue from the top of his head to the bottom of his spats. For this bear, every day is the Fourth of July. Flora's Santa Bear has a twinkle in his eye and a splendid red suit; he looks like he has just landed back at the North Pole after delivering presents to good little boys and girls around the world.

When Flora visited London a few years ago, she was fascinated by the Beefeaters at the Tower of London. Her Beefeater wears an exact replica of the guards' historic uniforms. Standing at attention with his staff in his paw, you can be sure that this teddy bear will keep order no matter what.

Mac Kendree is 12½ inches tall and jointed; he is made of mohair, with leather paws, and wears a ribbon bow.

Beefeater is 15 inches tall and jointed; he is made of acrylic-polyester fur, wears a wool uniform and a felt hat, and carries a staff.

Flora Mediate _____

Uncle Sam is 20 inches tall and jointed; he is made of alpaca and acrylic, and wears a cotton suit and hat.

Santa Bear is 17 inches tall and jointed; he is made of alpaca and wears a wool suit, with acrylic trim and a leather belt. He holds a felt bag.

Ted Menten

The teddy bears that live in Manhattan with Ted Menten are unlike teddy bears in the rest of the country. For one thing they are slim and have waistlines; for another they wear designer clothes. Ted's bear Columbine has appeared on the cover of a fashion magazine; his bear named Fashion models all the latest designs. According to her, hats and earrings will make a very big fashion statement for teddies in the coming season.

Ted has been making wonderful things ever since he was a small boy. He grew up in a family where make-believe was highly valued. Ted's dad designed mechanical window displays, his mom loved anything with a cat on it, and his grandmother adored dolls of all kinds. As a child Ted had his own puppet theatre and gave regular performances in playgrounds and libraries. He also had many teddy bears. Ted's First Bear recalls his childhood teddies, one of which had a penny sewed into its paw for good luck. First Bear also has a penny sewed under his paw pad.

Ted's first try at teddy-bear making was a result of a commission to design bear-making kits. While he was working on the designs for the kits, Ted decided he should actually make the bears himself. As so often happens with teddy bears, once he started making them he just couldn't seem to stop. Today Ted works almost exclusively with teddy bears; he designs and makes bears, draws a cartoon bear named HUG, and writes and edits magazines and books about teddy bears.

Columbine.

Columbine is 24 inches tall and jointed; she's made of mohair.

Fashion is 24 inches tall and jointed; she is made of mohair and wears a high-fashion, one-of-a-kind dress.

First Bear is 16 inches tall and jointed; he is made of mohair and wears a bow.

HUG and *HUG JR.* are made by the North American Bear Co. from Ted Menten's design.

Doris & Terry Michaud

Doris and Terry Michaud had been collecting old dolls and tin toys for many years when they came across the teddy bear that they call the Professor. He began accompanying the Michauds to toy shows, where they hung a sign around his neck that read, "Wanted: Old Teddy Bears." The Professor did not remain the Michauds' only bear for long. Just Ted joined them when his original owner approached Doris and Terry at a toy show and asked them to become the caretakers of the Ted bear that had been given to him when he was born in 1924. The Old Man's Bear was given to the Michauds by an elderly gentleman who was afraid that his family's new puppy might destroy his lifelong friend.

Doris and Terry have a teddy-bear museum. They write books about teddies and tell bear stories, and they even find time to make teddy bears that look a great deal like the old bears in their collection. The Professor, Just Ted, Eddie, and the Old Man's Bear have been reproduced many times; but the Michauds make their teddy bears with so much care and skill that they are very likely to become the antiques of tomorrow.

One of Doris's favorite bears is the Purse Bear, which is so small you always can bring him along for luck. He even wears a lucky heart charm. Doris often gives a Purse Bear to a friend who needs a little good luck. As Doris says, "Bears are a symbol of love."

Doris's Purse Bear (three shown) is 7 inches tall and jointed; she is made of acrylic plush and wears a necklace with a charm.

Eddie is 15 inches tall and jointed; he is made of a mohair blend and wears a collar and a bow tie.

Joanne Mitchell

A big sign hanging in Joanne Mitchell's work-room reads, "What's a family tree without a bear?" With the exception of Joanne's charming pairs of immigrant bears from Greece, Italy, Ireland, Germany, the Netherlands, and Poland, many of her bears look as though they fell off their family trees long ago. Joanne makes bag-lady bears. No two of her street-people bears are exactly alike, but each comes with the necessities of life on the street: an old hat; a soiled, baggy dress; long underwear; rolled-down stockings; birdseed to feed feathered friends; and shopping bags filled with precious odds and ends.

Joanne also makes a hobo bear. His name is Rusty. When he was new and fluffy, he was given to a man named Russell. The bear went along with him when he joined the marines. The privates in Company B made Rusty their mascot. While the soldiers were in the field all day, Rusty would sit on Russell's bunk quietly waiting. When Russell came back to the barracks at night, he'd give his bear a smile and a scratch on the ear, then pick up his harmonica and start to play. The nights were much better than the days for both the bear and the soldier. One evening Rusty's friend didn't return to the barracks. The guys in Company B dutifully sent the teddy bear back home, but nothing was ever the same for him again. Now Rusty roams the street with his possessions in his backpack and a harmonica and a tiny teddy bear in the pocket of his ragged overcoat.

Annie the Bag Lady *(two shown) is 18 inches tall and jointed; she is made of plush and carries two well-stocked paper shopping bags. No two Annies are exactly alike, but each comes dressed in a vintage hat, a worn-out dress, a top coat, long underwear, rolled-down stockings, and bunny slippers.*

Wizard of the Woodlands *is 22 inches tall and jointed; he is made of plush and wears a hooded cloak, a shirt, suede leggings, leather pouches, and a star-shaped amulet.*

Joanne Mitchell

Molly O'Bearigan (left) is 15 inches tall and jointed; she is made of mohair, wears a mop cap, a blouse, a vest, a petticoat, and a skirt, and carries a basket of dried wild flowers. *Patrick O'Bearigan* (right) is 16 inches tall and jointed; he is made of mohair, wears a cap, a scarf, and a vest, and carries a walking stick.

Rusty is 20 inches tall and jointed; he is made of plush and is dressed like a street person in ragged clothes, a cap, an overcoat, and a backpack.

Kathy Mullin

Like many bearmakers, Kathy Mullin made her first teddy as a present for her daughter. But once she had begun to make bears that she hoped to sell, Kathy's bear-making career took an unusual turn. The first place that sold Kathy's bears was a take-out restaurant with a teddy-bear theme. Rather than allowing her teddies to sit quietly on a shelf until someone bought them, the owner of the restaurant strung the teddy bears on fishing line, turning them into carnival bears whether they (or Kathy) liked it or not. Eventually all the bears sold, and Kathy now makes about 500 teddies a year.

Most Mulbeary's bears are classic teddies with long arms and close-set eyes. They need no further adornment than a basic ribbon bow, but two of her girl bears, Ophelia and Bear Peep, like to dress up. Ophelia wears pieces of the antique lace that Kathy collects whenever she can take time out from bear making to shop for fabrics in flea markets and antique shops. Bear Peep is a country bear dressed in her Sunday best. No two Bear Peeps are dressed alike because Kathy makes their hats and dresses from whatever scraps of lace and fabric she finds in her sewing box.

Another Mulbeary's bear, Aloysius, is a young sailor bear that's obviously on his first voyage. His little uniform is brand-new and the look on his face is a mixture of excitement and homesickness.

Aloysius is 13 inches tall and jointed; he is made of mohair and wears a cap and wool coat with braid trim and nautical buttons.

Ophelia is 22 inches tall and jointed; she is made of mohair and wears a christening dress with antique lace insets and a wreath made of dried and silk flowers, trimmed with ribbon. *Bear Peep* (two shown) is 8 inches tall and jointed; she is made of mohair and wears a cotton-print dress, an apron made from a handkerchief, and a floppy straw hat trimmed in lace and flowers.

Belinda & John Nesler

Belinda and John Nesler make teddy bears that look as though their fur has been hugged off and their ears have come loose from being used too often to lift the bears. Many of the Neslers' Raggy Taggy Teddies are missing eyes and have patched paws, but each of them has a story to tell.

A teddy bear named Sinclair was left behind in the attic when the boy who had loved him went off to college. The bear grew lonely and climbed down from the attic to go out into the world to search for new friends. He found Milo, a lost teddy bear with a lump in his cheek and a funny, lopsided grin. Sinclair also met up with a bear named Tobias; he had been an assistant engineer on a locomotive, but one day he fell out of the cab and was left lying on the railroad embankment. The bear known as Colonel Smudgery Doo came looking for the Raggy Taggy Teddies on his own. He had been discarded in a trash pile and figured that any place would be better than that, so he joined the other lost bears. This teddy-bear crew, along with Grand Pa Pa Jingles, has many adventures that Belinda writes and illustrates, using Jingles as her narrator.

The Neslers were dollmakers and teddy-bear collectors before they started making teddy bears. In addition to Raggy Taggy Teddies, they also make other bears that they call Aunt Addie's Golden Treasures.

Colonel Smudgery Doo *is 18 inches tall and jointed; he is made of synthetic fur and wears a military jacket, a belt, and a monocle.*

Left to right: ***Tobias*** *is 18 inches tall and wears overalls with a broken strap.* ***Sinclair*** *is 16 inches tall and wears a ribbon bow.* ***Milo*** *is 14 inches tall, wears a blue-jean jacket and straw hat, and carries a nap sack on a stick. They are jointed and made of synthetic fur.*

Gary & Margaret Nett

Margaret Nett is a professional seamstress who's been making stuffed animals for about 30 years. Her son Gary is a relative newcomer to teddy-bear making. They make perfectly crafted teddy bears in Gettysburg, Pennsylvania. The town's annual reenactment of the Civil War battle inspired the Netts to make bears dressed as a Confederate artillery major and a Union artillery sergeant. Gary carefully researched the uniforms so that they are totally authentic. The fabric Margaret uses to make the bears' uniforms is the same fabric that is used to make uniforms for the reenactment of the battle. Authentic belt buckles are cast to scale, and the soldier bears' historically correct shoes are made by a local cobbler.

The same high level of attention to detail goes into the Netts' 1928 Boy Scout Bear. The bear's embroidered badge sash is no more than six inches long, but every tiny badge is an exact replica of a real Boy Scout merit badge. The Scout also has just the right belt buckle and tie slide; even his shirt buttons are official Boy Scout issue.

One of the Netts' best-loved bears is Mr. Cinnamon Bear. He is an exact copy of the teddy bear featured in the story by Sara Tawney Leffertsby about a Steiff bear that came to the United States in 1907. Mr. Cinnamon Bear arrives in the nursery dressed in his Sunday best. He looks shy but brave, and seems to be hoping that the other toys and dolls will accept him.

Ruben is 10 inches tall and jointed; he is made of mohair and wears a bow tie.

Confederate Artillery Major Bear is 18 inches tall and jointed; his head and paws are made of mohair. The bear is authentically dressed in a wool uniform with brass buttons bearing the insignia "A" for artillery. The brass belt buckle on his leather belt has a "CS" insignia.

Mr. Teddy Roosevelt Bear is 18 inches tall and jointed; his head and paws are made of mohair, and he wears a wool morning suit, a cotton shirt, a silk tie, leather shoes, a top hat, and wire-frame glasses.

Mr. Cinnamon Bear is 18 inches tall and jointed; his head and paws are made of mohair. He wears a wool suit with short pants, a cotton shirt, a bow tie, velvet shoes, and knee socks.

Sue Newlin

In 1988 Sue Newlin was invited to come to Japan to teach a teddy-bear-making class at the Cuddly Brown Teddy Bear Shop in Tokyo. She was thrilled to be able to share the love and goodwill of teddy bears with 30 Japanese bearmakers. Many of her students stayed up all night after the class to finish their bears so that they would be able to show their teddies to Sue before she returned to the United States.

Sue is always designing and making new teddy bears, but most of the bears she makes are classic German-style teddy bears. Her traditional mohair bears include Jason, a chocolate-brown bear with claws; Oliver, a golden bear that looks worn; Gable, a shaggy pale-yellow bear; and Max, a bear that can be either rust or gold. One of Sue's bears, Scotty, is a departure from traditional teddy bears. Rather than stuffing him with excelsior, Sue stuffs Scotty with plastic beads so that he's cuddly and easily holds a pose.

Sue works in a room off her kitchen that's piled high with bolts of mohair and boxes of notions. She used to have several helpers who made teddy bears with her, but Sue felt uncomfortable sending out bears that she had not made totally herself. Sue works alone now, carefully handcrafting every teddy bear. Some of her bears are only five inches tall; others are as big as 25 inches. But all Sue's bears look you straight in the eye and pledge their lifelong devotion.

Sebastian is 24 inches tall and jointed; he's made of acrylic plush.

Bill is 16 inches tall and jointed; he's made of acrylic plush.

Kaylee Nilan

Most teddy bears are cuddly, cute, and lovable; but bears made by Kaylee Nilan are all that and more. Her bears stand on their own two feet, look you directly in the eye, and open their mouths in a friendly grin that quickly becomes a laugh. The bears from Beaver Valley might be mistaken for real bears if they were not wearing exquisite Victorian costumes. Their paws are leather, their claws are almost sharp, and their eyes are crafted so realistically that you can almost imagine them blinking from time to time.

Kaylee lives in a small town in the mountains of northern California. There's no traffic and no traffic lights, and sometimes a cub bear gets lost and wanders into town. With real bears living in the neighborhood, it's not surprising that Kaylee insists on such a high degree of realism in the stuffed animals she makes. When Kaylee is designing a bear, she carefully researches the animal, going into the woods to observe it in nature if she can. She also studies photographs as well as skeletal and dental charts. She learns as much as she can about the animal's behavior and habitat. Like animals in the wild, Kaylee's bears all live in families.

Many Beaver Valley bears have traveled a long way from their mountain home. One family is now living in the window of a health food store in Beverly Hills. The bears have been animated, and hardly anyone walks by without doing a double take when she sees what appear to be real bears that are elegantly dressed and making themselves at home in a store window.

Claire (left) is 22 inches tall; she is made of acrylic and is fully jointed, with a wooden armature and flexible arms. She wears a cotton dress with full sleeves, a white lace collar, ribbon sash, and a ruffled petticoat. *Zachary* (right) is made just like Claire, but he wears a wool jacket, with a shirt collar and tie.

Cyrus (papa bear) is 36 inches tall and fully jointed with a wooden armature; he is made of acrylic plush and wears a wool coat, a waistcoat, and a silk tie, and sports a fashionable cane (not shown). *Hallie* (mama bear) is made just like Cyrus, but she's dressed in a gored shirt, with a petticoat, and a flared jacket over a pleated silk collar, cuffs, and shirtfront. *Baby Bear* is 18 inches tall and jointed; she is made of acrylic plush and wears a cotton dress with ruffled yoke.

Kaylee Nilan _____

From left to right: **Baby Bear, Hallie, Zachary, Cyrus, and Claire**.

248

Kathy Olsen

If you had five children under the age of seven, as Kathy Olsen did, and you wanted them to have a very special teddy bear, you might find yourself learning to make bears, just as Kathy did. She remembered the durable, jointed teddy bear that she had when she was a child and knew that she wanted her children to have that kind of bear. But Kathy says, "Getting the idea to make bears was the easy part." She had trouble even finding the materials to make teddies, and she ended up writing lots of letters in search of patterns and sources for mohair.

After a frustrating search for just the right teddy-bear pattern, Kathy decided just to go ahead and make a bear. She experimented with several designs until she came up with Bosco Bear. He's a large teddy—22 inches tall—and he seems to have very clear ideas about who he is. As the first O.K. Bear, Bosco Bear is the leader of all the bears that have come after him. He can discuss any subject, and his favorite foods are honey, peanut butter, and cider, or so he tells Kathy.

As soon as she had made Bosco Bear, Kathy realized that she would have to make more bears. Five children were too much for one bear to keep happy. She made Nickerbear; he's a tough little bear that plays well with either a boy or a girl. Next Kathy designed Clariese; she's a little girl's dream bear. It wasn't long until each of the Olsen kids had an O.K. Bear, and their mom had become a bearmaker.

Bosco Bear is 22 inches tall and jointed; he is made of mohair and wears a satin ribbon.

Nickerbear is 14 inches tall and jointed; he is made of mohair, stuffed with excelsior, and has a growler.

Mary Olsen

Mary Olsen claims that she was born a teddy-bear collector. To prove this, she'll show you her baby book where a teddy bear is listed as one of her first Christmas presents. Mary will also show you the bear; her mother wisely saved Mary's first teddy for her until she was grown-up enough to want to care for him again. Her first bear is now just one teddy among a collection that has grown to include more than 300 bears, and Mary is a founder of a teddy-bear-collectors club where she and other teddy enthusiasts share friendship and their bears.

Mary made her first teddy bear from a kit. She worked on it all one rainy day and long into the night. Even though she was very tired by the time she finished the bear, when Mary looked into his face, she was thrilled. It wasn't long until Mary designed a bear of her own. She called him Gridley, and he looks like a kindergartner for whom everything is brand-new and very exciting. Mary has made more than 2,000 Gridleys. Some have gone off on daring adventures; some sit quietly on beds and display shelves; and other Gridleys are nationally famous models, appearing on greeting cards in all sorts of costumes. But in their little sawdust hearts, all of Mary's teddy bears carry a gentle goodness that comes from having been made with loving care.

Gridley.

Gridley is 11 inches tall and jointed; he is made of synthetic fur and wears a ribbon bow. The clothes and accessories shown were provided by the photographer.

Donna Focardi Pedini

Donna Focardi Pedini searches out wool coats at garage sales. When she finds a coat that's the right color, she cuts it up into small pieces to make miniature teddy bears. Donna often makes a bear for a friend or relative to commemorate an important occasion or to hold a treasured memory. She also makes bears to trade with other artists and craftspeople for their work. Indian and Papoose were made to trade for a watercolor painting of a horse. She traded one of her Golfer Bears for wool fabric from which she has made other teddy bears.

Donna designed the first Fisherman Bear for her father, who's an avid fisherman. Hiker Bear was made for her brother, who's a geologist and loves the outdoors. Good memories and affection inspire Donna's bears, but once the prototype has been made the teddies themselves often inspire Donna to make additional bears. Gold Wool Bear is just a plain wool teddy, but Donna fell in love with him and was unable to send him out into the world, so she felt she had to go on making this little teddy.

Donna had expected to use her college degree in stable and farm management after she graduated. But she got involved in making teddy bears and has yet to get out on the farm. Since 1982 Donna has designed more than 100 teddy bears; she says she's just getting started.

Golfer Bear is 6 inches tall and jointed; he is made of upholstery fabric, wears a vest, knickers, a hat, and glasses, and carries a golf bag with clubs.

Fisherman Bear, Hiker Bear, and *Indian and Papoose* are 6 inches tall and jointed; they're made of upholstery fabric. *Fisherman* wears felt clothes and comes with a pole, a reel, a net, a pipe, and a fishing license. *Hiker* comes with a knit hat, scarf, backpack, and a walking stick. *Indian* wears deerskin, beads, and feathers.

Rose Policky

Rose Policky has made well over a thousand bears. No two are exactly alike, and most of her teddy bears are less than one and a half inches tall. An Itty Bitty Buddy is made from 18 tiny pieces of Ultrasuede. With amazing patience and attention to detail, Rose shapes the little bits of fabric into a charming, endearing bear.

Many of Rose's bears live in dollhouses; but some ride around in pockets to give their human friends a little extra confidence during board meetings, dental appointments, and final exams. Rose once made a bear for a young soldier in boot camp. He wanted to have a teddy bear to keep him company while he was away from home, but he only had an 18-inch by 18-inch drawer in which to store all his personal possessions. To fill his request, Rose called up one of her bravest Itty Bitty Buddies, and he's in the army now.

After Rose made her first teddy, she showed it to her son. He looked at it for a moment and said, "That's a nice kangaroo, Mom." With practice and patience, Rose perfected her bear making. No one would ever confuse Brandon T. Bear with a kangaroo. He's only two inches tall, but he wears top hat and tails, and behind his back Brandon carries a bunch of silk flowers for the little lady bear he's courting. Recently Rose has been making a big bear. Wagger B. Bear is a whopping five inches tall. Even though he's more than twice the size of most of her bears, Rose thinks of Wagger as a whimsical child.

Brandon T. Bear is 2 inches tall and jointed; he's made of Ultrasuede. Brandon sometimes wears a top hat and tails, and carries three silk roses (not shown).

Itty Bitty Buddies are 1/2, 3/4, 7/8, 1 1/8, and 1 1/2 inches tall and jointed; they are made of Ultrasuede and have ribbon bows.

Beverly & Kimberlee Port

Beverly Port began collecting and making teddy bears back when most people were unwilling to admit that they had never outgrown teddy bears. She passed on her love of bears to her daughter, Kimberlee, who began making teddies when she was 13. She now makes her own distinctive miniature bears. One of her favorite childhood toys was the Steiff bear her mother gave her when she was four. Kimberlee called the three-inch bear Bitsy, and every night she clutched him tightly in her hand while she fell asleep.

Kimberlee says that making a bear from tiny scraps of material is an amazing experience. With old Bitsy looking on from her place on the shelf in the workroom, Kimberlee shapes her Bitsy Bears. One bear is a clown; another is Bearlerina, a bear that stands on point. Teddy, Teddy Tree is a teddy bear that has been transformed into a Christmas tree. His green body is decorated with 50 miniature ornaments and tiny blinking lights.

Beverly calls her bears Time Machine Teddies. One special little bear is known as Scraps. He's a keeper of memories. The teddy looks as though he was made of sewing scraps, and he carries a bag in which Beverly tucks the first teddy-bear pattern she ever made. There is also room in his bag for your own memories and keepsakes, which you can be sure Scraps will cherish.

Kimbearlee Port Kreations from left to right: **Rusty, Fifi,** *and* **T.T. Rusty** *and* **T.T.** *are 7 inches tall, fully jointed, and made of vintage mohair.* **Fifi** *is 8 inches tall and jointed, and wears a costume of handmade lace and embroidery.*

Beverly Port's bear **Miss Emily** *is 18 inches tall and jointed; she is made of vintage mohair and wears an organdy dress and a silk hat.*

*Beverly's **La Petit Victoria** is 20 inches tall. She has armature arms and legs, and a swivel waist. This mohair bear wears an antique jet-beaded bodice over a satin dress.*

*Kimberlee's **Teddy, Teddy Tree** is 10 inches tall and fully jointed with a swivel neck; he is made of mohair, has shoebutton eyes, one-of-a-kind ornaments, and tiny lights. **Santa Claus Bear** is 6 inches tall, jointed, and made of vintage fabrics.*

Cynthia Powell

Cynthia Powell makes wonderful little bears with painstaking skill. She carefully sews perfect replicas of full-size teddy bears by hand. Each teddy is made from at least 19 pieces of fabric. Basic Bear is a traditional bear with a shaved muzzle, a pouchy tummy, and little arms just long enough to give you a tiny bear hug.

Since Cynthia is a jewelry designer, she is accustomed to working on a very small scale, but her Tiny Bear is a challenge to make even so. He is only one and a quarter inches tall. Cynthia must be especially careful when she places Tiny Bear's eyes and nose; the placement of these features brings the bear to life. If his face isn't put on just right, a miniature bear can look mean or scary. But Tiny Bear always looks sweet and thoughtful.

Cynthia's Ballerina Bear poses on point in her little leather ballet slippers. She wears silk and ribbons, and is the envy of all Cynthia's other bears. Even her Antique-Look Bear admires the ballerina's youth and joie de vivre. He's an old-fashioned teddy bear that looks a little worn and very wise.

Cynthia's Muff Bear is a special little creature. She's only one and three-quarters inches tall, but around her neck she wears a white teddy-bear muff that's a perfect miniature of the muffs that little girls used to wear.

*Top row left to right: **Basic Bear, Ballerina Bear,** and **Antique-Look Bear;** they are 1¾ inches tall and jointed. Bottom row: Two **Tiny Bears;** they are 1¼ inches tall and jointed. The bears are made of nylon velvet, with leather paws. **Ballerina Bear** wears a net tutu, silk ribbons, and Ultrasuede ballet slippers.*

*Top to bottom: **Basic Bear, Bunny Bear,** and two **Tiny Bears. Bunny Bear** is 1¾ inches tall and jointed; he is made of nylon velvet, with leather bunny ears and a cotton-lace collar, and carries a basket of dyed eggs.*

Betsy Reum

Tinker (two shown) is 7 inches tall and jointed; she is made of mohair, has glass eyes, and wears a bow. **Penny** is 6 inches tall and jointed; she is made of mohair and wears a bow.

Betsy Reum had always thought of herself as a person who preferred dolls to stuffed toys, but after her sons were born and she began buying teddy bears for them, Betsy found herself gradually shifting away from dolls and starting her own bear collection. It took her more than a year to make her first teddy bear. His name is Toby, and he now sits in a corner of Betsy's sewing room, keeping her company and watching her make one new teddy bear after another.

Betsy's teddies Prescott and Priscilla are like a couple of schoolchildren. He is gawky, with gangly elbows and big feet. She is coy, with soft brown eyes and a silk bonnet. Her bear Thomas is a fatherly sort of bear. But of all her teddy bears, Betsy's favorite is the Puppeteer. Betsy's sister collects anything that has to do with the puppets Punch and Judy, and she suggested that Betsy make a puppeteer bear. The teddy bear has a puppet on each paw; he takes his portable stage from village to village, entertaining everyone with his show.

Betsy studied clothing and textiles in college, but she says that she has learned about making bears from the teddy bears themselves. Now that her children are in school all day, Betsy has become a full-time bearmaker, sewing elaborate Puppeteers, as well as Tinker, Toby, and Thomas—teddies that are simply cuddly bears.

The **Puppeteer** is 15 inches tall and jointed; he is made of mohair, wears a wool cloak, and carries two satin puppets with clay heads and a wooden stage.

Saki Romerhaus

When Saki Romerhaus designed Aunt Lydia, her well-loved bear, she put a lot of herself into her creation. The bear is an old-fashioned peddler, traveling the world to collect and sell fancy goods. Aunt Lydia's imaginary adventures are based on Saki's extensive travels in Europe and throughout the United States, accumulating antique lace, ribbon, and fabrics. Her lifelong love of fine fabrics and handmade decorations inspires Saki when she makes Romerhaus Bears and their exquisite clothes. Aunt Lydia's attire is elaborately detailed. The bear is dressed in Victorian eyelet and antique calico; she wears leather, high-button baby shoes and carries a handmade basket filled with silk thread, ornamental buttons, notions, and other precious things.

Saki's first bear, Baby Bruno, was cute and chubby. But Saki was not satisfied; she wanted to make bears that could wear clothes and take on more personality. She changed her design, lengthening the bear's nose, body, and legs, and extending and curving its arms; Saki had created the forebear of the Romerhaus clan.

The Romerhaus Bears are country folk dressed in beautiful old fabrics. Saki makes hats, ear wreaths, and crowns from herbs and everlasting flowers for her bears. Many Romerhaus Bears come with miniature baskets, shoes, and tiny quilts. Each bear has a small hand-cut heart attached to its lower back on which Saki writes the series the bear is part of, the materials it's made of, copyright date, the date made, and the bear's number.

Sarah Romerhaus Bear (left) is 8 inches tall and jointed; she's made of acrylic and wears a lace collar. **Berta Deutsch Choklat Romerhaus Bear** (standing) is 14 inches tall and jointed; she's made of acrylic and wears an apron made from a quilt, a heart pendant, and an ear wreath. **Friedrich Deutsch Choklat Romerhaus Bear** (right) is 8 inches tall and jointed; he is made of acrylic and wears a bib made from an old quilt.

Wilhelmina HoneyWunsch (standing) is 14 inches tall and jointed; she is made of merino wool and wears a pinafore with ribbon trim. **Frieda HoneyWunsch** (right) is 8 inches tall and jointed; she is made of merino wool and wears a lace collar and crown.

267

Emily Romerhaus Bear (standing) is 14 inches tall and jointed; she is made of acrylic and wears a dress and apron made from antique fabric. She wears a straw hat decorated with dried flowers and carries a basket. **Gerta WunschBaer Romerhaus Bear** (two shown in front) is 8 inches tall and jointed; she is made of German mohair and wears clothes made from antique fabric. **Baby Jason** is 8 inches tall and jointed; he is made of acrylic and wears a bib.

Fritz HoneyWunsch (left) is 8 inches tall and jointed; he is made of merino wool and carries an antique quilt for a security blanket. **Wilhelmina** (standing) and **Frieda** (right) **HoneyWunsch.** Wilhelmina wears a capelet and flower crown.

Saki Romerhaus

Standing left to right: **Very Special Edition Astarte Phoebe Edelweiss** (11 inches); **Wilhelmina HoneyWunsch** (14 inches); **Katrina Edelweiss** (14 inches); **Very Special Edition Aunt Lydia Edelweiss, the Peddler,** (14 inches); and **Thea Edelweiss** (14 inches). Sitting left to right: **Monika HoneyWunsch** (8 inches) and **Very Special Edition Baby Heika Edelweiss** (8 inches). **Aunt Lydia** is dressed entirely in antique fabric and wears high-button baby shoes. She comes with an egg basket and a larger basket that contain wooden spools of thread, buttons, and pieces of tatting and lace. Aunt Lydia also has a tin-reinforced, pressed-paper box, an old fabric purse, a glass-domed dish, scissors, and a needle holder with antique needles.

Kathy & Owen Sandusky

Kathy and Owen Sandusky don't make the kind of bears that like to sit quietly on a shelf and watch the world go by. Their bear Happy Wanderer is ready to take off on an adventure. He's warmly dressed and wears comfortable walking boots. The bear even has his walking stick in paw. Wee Wanderer is a smaller version of this handsome bear.

Kathy and Owen both have full-time jobs, but they manage to make about 30 teddy bears a month. To meet this production schedule, Kathy takes a partially finished teddy bear to her office to work on during lunch. The Sanduskys divide the bear-making process, so that each of them has different tasks. Kathy designs the bears and sews their clothes. Owen cuts the fabric, stuffs the teddies, and packs the bears to be shipped to their new homes. In addition to the Wanderer bears, the Sanduskys make a baby-girl bear called Gretchen. She is about the size of a small baby, and each Gretchen is dressed in an antique baby dress.

Owen's favorite teddy is Happy Wanderer because he seems to have such a positive attitude about life. Kathy prefers a large dark-brown bear called Chester. He is named for an Alaskan brown bear that used to live in the San Diego Zoo. The Sandusky children were very fond of Chester and would visit him often to watch him perform his tricks.

Wee Wanderer is 12 inches tall and jointed; he is made of mohair, has glass eyes, and wears a wool jacket, boots, and a hat. He carries a walking stick.

Happy Wanderer (two shown) is 17 inches tall and jointed; he is made of acrylic and wears a wool jacket, boots, and a hat with a feather. He holds a walking stick.

Laurie Sasaki

Laurie Sasaki says that she started making teddy bears to support her bear-collecting habit. She couldn't stop buying teddies and she was quickly running out of cash, so Laurie took the logical step of using her long-idle sewing skills to become a bearmaker.

Laurie's first teddy bears were average-size bears made of acrylic plush. But after she took a workshop on making miniature bears from Elaine Fujita-Gamble, Laurie began to concentrate on tiny teddies. Laurie's No-No Teddy Baby is three and a half inches tall, and her Santa is a mere two and a quarter inches tall. But like all of Laurie's bears, these miniatures are patterned after traditional teddy bears. Teddy Baby is a yes-no bear; he looks and acts very much like his ancestor—a Schuco bear of the same name. When you move his tail from side to side, Teddy Baby shakes his head "no." Another of Laurie's novel bears is called Flower Bear; the bear's head unscrews to reveal a perfume bottle that's hidden inside her body. Laurie also makes bellhops, jesters, and the five-member Bearrie Patch All-Teddy Band. Each bear is perfectly detailed and costumed.

Sometimes Laurie can't resist making a large bear. She'll find a piece of antique mohair and make a bear that looks like one of the old bears she would like to have for her collection. These big teddy bears, such as Buster and Chester, look as though a child has already loved off much of their fur.

No-No Teddy Baby *(two shown) is 3½ inches tall and jointed; he is made of mohair and cotton velvet, and wears a leather collar.*

Buster *is 13 inches tall and jointed; he is made of distressed mohair, has shoe-button eyes, and wears a tie.*

The members of the **Bearrie Patch All-Teddy Band** are 4½ inches tall without their hats; they are jointed, made of upholstery mohair, and dressed in band uniforms and hats with braid trim and feathers. Each musician carries an instrument.

Jester Bear is 4½ inches tall—not including his hat—and jointed; he's made of mohair that's dyed to make his costume, with a lace ruff and braid trim.

Steve Schutt

Steve Schutt makes bears with so much love and attention to detail that they almost seem to be alive or—in the case of his bear Tipton—dead. Steve once stowed this three-foot-tall teddy bear in the overhead locker on an airplane. The bear was covered with a plastic garbage sack, but the bag was too small for Tipton, and his legs and antique shoes were left sticking out. Before the plane took off, the captain was alerted by an observant flight attendant that a body had been carried on to the plane. He came back to Steve's seat and demanded an explanation. Everyone had a good laugh, but Tipton now travels in the baggage compartment.

Steve's first teddy bears were really puppets. He had been making puppets for about 25 years, and these hybrid bear/puppets helped him make the transition to a new medium. After the strings came off the teddies, Steve made a series of bears that were careful copies of antique teddy bears. He made them so well that some of his bears were sold as real antiques. This fraudulent use of his teddies determined Steve to design and make bears that are distinctively his own.

Many of Steve's Bear-"S"-Ence bears are long-legged and exceptionally tall. They're dressed in vintage clothes and wear leather shoes. Their knees can be bent so that they're able to sit comfortably in a chair or ride a tricycle. But the most distinctive quality of Steve's bears is the way they all seem to convey their maker's personality.

Borg *is 14 inches tall and jointed; he is made of antique mohair and wears a collar with a tie.*

Santa Bear *is 18 inches tall and jointed; he is made of new mohair, and his fur is dyed to make his costume. **Noel** is 10 inches tall and jointed; he is made of antique mohair and has shoe-button eyes and a ribbon bow.*

Thurston is 18 inches tall and jointed; he is made of synthetic coat lining and wears only a bow (not shown). The clothes and accessories were provided by the photographer.

Reggie is 18 inches tall and jointed; he is made of mohair and wears a coat, a scarf, and a hood from Tailor Made Togs for Teddies.

Ansel is 12 inches tall and jointed; he's made of mohair.

Tucker is about 36 inches tall and jointed; he is made of antique horsehair and wears antique clothes, shoes, and glasses.

283

Denis Shaw makes about 75 different teddy bears, and no two bears are exactly the same. There are no twins in Denis's Den because he never makes a particular bear until the bear that the new one will resemble has already left Denis's shop. Denis thinks of bears as individuals. When he finishes a bear, he always gives it a big hug to bring it to life.

The first bear that Denis made came out looking dazed and bewildered. Most of Denis's friends said that the bear looked like the kind of teddy only a mother could love. When another friend saw the bear, she knew immediately that he needed her and took the teddy bear home.

Denis says that he makes so many different kinds of bears because there are so many different people who need and want teddy bears. Sherlock is a small teddy that appeals to people who like an independent type of bear. Bosco Bear is made for people who like real bears; he's modeled after a bear Denis enjoys watching at the zoo. Fisby is a dreamer, and Dozey is only half awake.

Denis also makes an unusually simple, nearly flat teddy bear that he calls Kuki, the Cookie Cutter Bear. His high-stepping walk gives him an arrogant look. Some people think he looks like a Yuppie and should carry a briefcase. Denis likes to think of him adding life to a Christmas tree by pretending to be an ornament.

Sherlock is 7 inches tall and has jointed arms and legs; he is made of upholstery fabric, has plastic safety eyes, and wears a bow tie.

Fisby (left) is 8 inches tall and has jointed arms and legs; he is made of mohair and upholstery fabric. *Dozey* (right) is 10 inches tall and unjointed; he's made of synthetic fur and Ultrasuede.

Denis Shaw ———————————

Kuki *(eight shown) is 8 inches tall and unjointed; he is made of upholstery fabric and wears a crocheted scarf.*

Linda Suzanne Shum

Edward (left) is 20 inches tall and jointed; he is made of distressed wool, wears a sailor hat and coat, and carries a tin replica of a zeppelin. *Cullen* (center). *Country Jesting* (right) is 12 inches tall and jointed; he is made of mohair that's dyed to make his motley, wears a hat and a ruff, and carries a puppet.

Almost as soon as she opened her husband's Christmas present and looked into the eyes of her first teddy bear, Linda Suzanne Shum knew that she was going to become a teddy-bear designer. All through high school, she had been primarily interested in arts and crafts, but at college Linda took a business degree. The Christmas teddy bear helped her pull her divergent backgrounds together.

Linda calls her teddy-bear business Ted E. Tail Originals, and she designs and makes bears that she feels reflect her love for all living things. Linda's bear Cullen is a relaxed, happy fellow with a heart-shaped embroidered nose and an easy way about him. His shoulders are drawn up and his head is tucked as if he's saying, ''What will be, will be.''

Country Jesting is a bear with heart; in fact, Linda ties two hearts around his neck—the better to make dreams come true. Her classic teddy bear, Edward, looks like he came off the pages of an antique storybook. He holds a model of a 1928 zeppelin, which helps him remember life the way it used to be lived. For Linda, Edward is a symbol of childhood and the child in all of us. Although Linda never had a teddy bear of her own while she was a little girl, she believes in the magic of teddy bears and hopes that her bears bring joy to the hearts of everyone who holds them.

Cullen is 15 inches tall and jointed; he is made of mohair, with Ultrasuede paws and glass eyes, and wears a bow.

Marcia Sibol can't remember when she first started sewing. As a small child she made doll clothes; later she made her own clothes. As an adult she's made her living as a dressmaker. Marcia's skilled hand is evident in every teddy bear she now makes.

Maggie Rose is dressed in a teal-blue taffeta gown trimmed in Chantilly lace. Marcia's attention to detail is unsurpassed, and she has spent many hours sewing on scads of seed pearls by hand. The bear is also exquisitely made and has just the right degree of dignity for a genteel lady. Katherine is a sophisticated matron bear in a lace and chiffon gown with handstitched beading. Her eyes and the set of her mouth let you know that Katherine is a bit fussy and insists that Marcia save the best gowns for her. Not all of Marcia's bears are grand ladies. Goodhard and Prudence are country children in simple cotton clothes. Cinnamon is an elegant bear that doesn't need clothes to establish his identity as someone you can trust with your secrets.

While teddy bears may be the great love of Marcia's life, she is also especially fond of baby squirrels—the real kind. Humane societies bring sick and abandoned babies to Marcia, who bottle-feeds the tiny squirrels and nurses them back to health. One of her teddy bears helps Marcia care for the squirrels. She's an old bear with a long, full skirt; and Marcia puts her in the cage with the squirrels, who climb under the bear's skirt and huddle close to her safe fur.

Cinnamon and *Serenity* are 15½ inches tall and jointed; they are made of mohair and wear lace cuffs and matching ear bows.

Katherine is 15 inches tall and jointed; she is made of plush and wears lace and chiffon over organza and taffeta. Her lace hat is trimmed with flowers and net bows, and she carries a lace-covered parasol.

Fred Slayter

After 20 years in the antique business, Fred Slayter decided he needed a change of pace; he bought a 100-year-old ski lodge. He and his partner Joyce Martin had great expectations for the success of their new venture. If it had snowed that winter, Fred might not be making Paisley Bears today. But there was no snow and no skiers. After sitting around for several months watching the money drain out of his bank account, Fred decided he had to do something. He took down a paisley shawl that was hanging on the wall and cut out a bear, using an old Steiff teddy as a pattern. One bear led to another, and Fred eventually gave up on the ski lodge; he and Joyce have been making teddy bears ever since.

Paisley Bears are made entirely from antique hand-woven fabric; the bears are crafted to use the bold pattern of the paisley to its best advantage. Before they cut out a Paisley Bear, Fred and Joyce study the fabric to find the patterns that will form the bear's features. When they sew up the teddy, they are careful to match the seams perfectly.

Not all of Fred's bears are made from paisley shawls; some are made from plush and only accented with the fabric. Werner is a plush bear with a paisley tie; he keeps his paws stuffed deep in his pockets. When he makes the bear he calls The Preacher Himself, Fred limits his use of paisley to the appliqué on the bear's stole. Pee Paw and Greystone have paisley paw pads.

The Preacher Himself is 22 inches tall and jointed; he is made of plush and wears a shirt, a liturgical collar, and a stole with paisley appliqués.

Paisley Bears are 26, 16, and 6 inches tall and jointed; they are made of antique hand-woven paisley and have velvet bows.

Sally Stearns

When a new Stearnsy Bear is completed, Sally Stearns's son gives it a hard squeeze to get its heart going. Sally calls her bears "people bears," and they seem to be alive with love. Almost all of the Stearnsy Bears are dressed, and Sally likes to use castoffs as a way of keeping her nostalgic teddies in touch with the past. A bit of clothing often sparks the development of a new bear because it reminds Sally of someone she once knew, a member of her family, or a local character. Her grandfather is remembered by the bear O.P. Brite. Two fisherman bears, Punk and Arlie, are modeled after two men who live in Sally's hometown, Stotts City, Missouri.

Many of Sally's bears also remind other people of friends and relatives. After she made Song Leader Bear, Sally placed a hymnal in the bear's paws and opened it to a favorite old song. The woman who bought the bear was especially moved by this charming fellow because the song he was singing had been her grandmother's favorite hymn.

Sally has a special affection for people living through hard times. Her bag-lady bears may be down in the heels, but they are obviously making the best of a bad situation. Birdie shares bits of bread with the birds in the park, and Sally's other street-people bears also seem to be committed to finding happiness wherever they are.

Willard is 11 inches tall and jointed; he is made of synthetic fur and wears pants, a coat, a tie, and a derby.

Punk and *Arlie* are 22 inches tall and jointed; they are made of synthetic fur and wear overalls and straw hats.

Birdie *is 22 inches tall and jointed; she is made of synthetic fur and wears a dress, a hat, a sweater, and a hodgepodge of collectibles.*

Elizabeth *and* ***Victoria*** *are 22 inches tall and jointed; they are made of synthetic fur and wear crepe and velvet dresses.*

Max and *Leila* are 22 inches tall and jointed; they're made of synthetic fur. He wears pants and a matching vest, a shirt with garters on the sleeves, and a tie. She wears an evening dress and lots of jewelry.

Pocohontas is 20 inches tall and unjointed; he is made of synthetic fur and carries a white flag.

Judith Swanson

Judith Swanson makes teddy bears out of real fur. Each of her bears is different from the others because Judith finds her inspiration to make a teddy bear in the fur itself. She shapes her bear designs to use the fur to its best advantage.

Working with real fur is much more difficult than working with fur fabric, such as alpaca or mohair. Each pattern piece must be placed on the pelt in exactly the right place, or the bear's coat will stick out in all directions. Judith's Fur Real Bears are all perfectly crafted; they seem to insist that you pick them up and cuddle them. Judith molds a teddy bear's face after she has made the rest of the bear. She has a special way of shaping the nose, cheeks, and jaws that puts life into the bear's face. After Judith completes a bear, she names the teddy and gives him or her a "bearology" listing his forebears. There's even a place to enter the date of the bear's adoption.

One of Judith's special teddies is named Snow Bear. He is made from a long-hair, polar-sheep pelt. This large bear has suede paws. He looks as though he would feel right at home at the North Pole, but once you've touched his luxurious fur, you may think that he should come home with you and cuddle up on a cold winter's night.

Scooter is 11 inches tall and jointed; he is made of mink and wears a bow.

Muffins is 18 inches tall and jointed; he is made of sheared beaver, has button eyes, and wears a bow.

Laura Walker has been collecting bears and stuffed animals ever since she was a little girl. For her the teddy bear is a universal symbol of love. Laura's teddies can cross any barrier to deliver a message of love and caring. You can tell by the names Laura gives her teddy bears that they are all very special to her. Most of Laura's bears have the kind of names that mothers call their own children when they're tucking them in for the night; three of Laura's bears are named Puddin', Sweetie, and Buddy.

Spike is another of Laura's bears; he's a spunky bear, full of mischief, and always looking for fun. Puddin' is a little-girl bear; she may dress in prim white cotton and ribbons, but that doesn't mean she won't shinny up a tree every time she gets a chance. Priscilla is a pretty pink bear that has sparkling black eyes and wears a fancy lace collar.

Laura calls her bear-making company The Nine Acre Woods. The name is a reference to Winnie-the-Pooh's Hundred Acre Wood, and Laura hopes that her bears convey some of the same tender understanding that makes Pooh so lovable. Laura works in her home while she takes care of her three children. She often asks them to stop playing with their teddy bears and help her stuff a teddy. Her sons are willing to help because they seem to understand that bear making is important work since bears help people to be happy.

Spike.

Puddin' (left) is 24 inches tall and jointed; she is made of mohair and wears a doll's cotton dress. *Spike* (center) is 12 inches tall and jointed; he is made of mohair and wears a bow. *Priscilla* (right) is 16 inches tall and jointed; she is made of mohair and wears a lace collar.

Kathleen Wallace

By the time Kathleen Wallace made her first teddy bear, she was an accomplished seamstress who had made just about everything you can make with fabric and thread except teddy bears. Kathleen made that original bear just to see if she could do it. Although the blue-and-white ticking bear she made is not much to look at compared with the teddies Kathleen makes today, she was proud of him and decided to go on sewing teddy bears.

After experimenting with several kinds of bears, Kathleen realized that making traditional teddies gave her the greatest satisfaction. She is currently making bears with center seams that closely resemble the bears that used to be made by Steiff. The design for this kind of bear was developed for its economical use of materials. Ends of fabric are pieced together to make the center piece of the teddy bear's head. Wally, Kathleen's 22-inch center-seam teddy, and his smaller pal, Honey B, are not only historically accurate, but they are also the heirs to the love that generations of children have given their teddy bears.

Uncle Maxwell and Aunt Beartha have the special look that you usually see only in classic and well-loved teddies. His eyes shine with love, and she is quick to offer a helping paw and a kind ear. The couple's favorite nephew, Little Max, is a mischievous cub, but his uncle believes that with enough love he'll grow up to be a real gentlebear.

Little Max.

Uncle Maxwell is 24 inches tall, Aunt Beartha is 20 inches tall, and Little Max is 18 inches tall. They are jointed and made of mohair. Maxwell wears antique eyeglasses and a collar. Beartha wears a lace collar with a broach, and Little Max wears a ribbon bow.

Carol-Lynn Rössel Waugh

Carol-Lynn Rössel Waugh doesn't have time anymore to make many bears. In addition to making teddies, she's a writer and photographer whose favorite topic is teddy bears. Many of the teddy bears that Carol-Lynn has made lately never leave home, except when she takes a teddy along with her when she travels.

The first bear that Carol-Lynn created is called Yetta Nother Bear. Before she had finished working on Yetta, Carol-Lynn had made her a trunkful of clothes and given her a family of ten other teddy bears. Yetta's mother, Caroline, is a sweet intellectual bear that's interested in genealogy and runs a dancing school. Her father, Frederick Olmstead Bear, writes fantasy mysteries and often wears a Dick Tracy pin. Yetta is now manufactured in England by the House of Nisbet, and she is the most requested bear the company has ever made.

Although she's recently made a fairly large teddy named Marmalade Bear, Carol-Lynn likes to make six-inch bears, such as Grenadine and Cinnamon, because they are easy to conceal in a pocket or purse. Carol-Lynn believes that if you bring a teddy bear along with you, your bear will make people smile and feel just a little bit better about themselves. She also likes to make bears in twos because they're much less lonely. Her bears Dandy and Amber both have the same white fur, but Carol-Lynn can easily tell them apart—Dandy is the one with the blue ribbon.

Cinnamon and *Grenadine* are 6 inches tall and jointed; they are made of mohair and wear ribbon bows, lace collars, and heart pendants.

Amber and *Dandy* are 16 inches tall and fully jointed; they are made of German mohair, have antique shoe-button eyes, and wear ribbon bows.

Yetta Nother Bear is 11 inches tall and fully jointed; she is made of German mohair and is sold unclothed.

Yetta Nother Bear.

Beverly White

While Beverly White was growing up, her favorite book was a volume of short biographies of American heros and heroines. Today she makes teddy bears dressed like the patriots she enjoyed reading about. Beverly's bears are not serious representations; they're more like children dressed up for a class play. One of her camel-colored bears plays Betsy Ross, another is Ben Franklin, and a third takes the part of Thomas Jefferson. Betsy Bear holds an unfinished flag; there's a star on her paw that she's getting ready to sew on. Ben Bear has a kite with a key on the string. Even though the bear wears wire-rim glasses, you can't help but think of him as a child playing the part of the famous inventor and statesman. Beverly's Thom Jefferson Bear holds a miniature copy of the Declaration of Independence in one paw and a quill pen in the other.

Beverly also makes bears that did not play a major role in United States history. Willie, the Broadstreet Bully, is a tough little bear in knickers that rolls a hoop down the sidewalk in summer and slides a hockey puck across the ice in winter.

Before she made teddy bears, Beverly made traditional clothes-pin dolls. Many of her bears are costumed in the same way as some of her dolls. Beverly says they look almost like twins, but as the mother of two sets of twins, she might be inclined to see double.

Willie, the Broadstreet Bully, is 12 inches tall and jointed; he is made of mohair, wears a wool cap and shorts, and rolls a hoop with a stick.

Betsy Bear, Ben Bear, and *Thom Jefferson Bear* are 11 inches tall and jointed; they are made of wool fabric and dressed in cotton clothes. *Betsy* wears a dress, an apron, and a bonnet and carries a partially completed 13-star flag. *Ben* wears knee britches and a shirt, and carries a paper kite with a wooden key on the string. *Thom* wears knickers, a vest, and a shirt, and carries a reduced copy of the Declaration of Independence and a quill pen.

Barbara Wiltrout

For many years Barbara Wiltrout collected antique dolls and old toys, especially mechanical toys. She never paid much attention to teddy bears until she began raising cocker spaniels for show. Her interest in dogs sparked an interest in stuffed animals. She started collecting antique teddies, and this led her to designing her own bears. Barbara calls her bear-making company Kaleb Designs. "Kaleb" means faithful, friendly, and affectionate; and Barbara insists that all her bears have these qualities before she lets them leave her shop and go out into the world.

Barbara's bears have a special look that says that they are patient and faithful. Barbara achieves this look by using a technique that she learned while showing her dogs. She gives each bear a show trim, clipping its muzzle by hand until it looks just right. Since many of Barbara's bears are quite large—over two feet tall—shaping a bear's face to create a distinctive personality can take many hours of careful work.

A bear Barbara calls Linus looks like a Depression-era farm boy when he wears his overalls and a cap. He's a mechanical yes-no bear and shakes his head to agree or to disagree when you move his tail. Barbara's husband, who restores antique cars, makes the bear's mechanism from antique-car parts. Another of Barbara's bears stands on all fours on wheels; he indicates with a kind look that he welcomes other little bears to climb on his back for a ride.

Bear on Wheels is 18 inches tall and 24 inches long, and has a jointed head; he is made of mohair and has metal wheels.

Shadrack (left) is 32 inches tall and fully jointed; he is made of German mohair and wears a bellhop uniform or a raincoat and hat (not shown). *Linus* (right) is 28 inches tall and jointed; he is made of mohair and wears a bellhop uniform, overalls and a cap (shown on following page), a raincoat and a hat (not shown), or a clown suit (not shown).

Linus is 28 inches tall and jointed; he is made of mohair and wears overalls and a cap.

Bear is 16 inches tall and jointed; he is made of mohair, with felt paws and shoe-button eyes. This bear is a replica of a 1904 Steiff bear.

Joan & Mike Woessner

Teddy-bear making moved quickly from being just a hobby for Joan and Mike Woessner to being their full-time work. Joan had been writing books on crafts and teaching classes; but as soon as she realized how much she enjoyed making teddies, she sold her share in her craft store to her partner and set up a workshop at home. Mike soon joined Joan in the studio, where they often put in 17-hour days. But both the Woessners say they've never been happier. Mike cuts out the fabric, stuffs arms and legs, and joints the bears. Joan designs the bears and sews their heads and faces. She gives no two bears exactly the same face and limits production of each teddy bear she designs to 100 bears.

The Woessners call they company Bear Elegance Exclusives, and most of their bears are designed to be able to hold a pose. They're traditionally jointed teddies that are stuffed with beads so that they can be molded to stay in any stance. Amy is a soft baby bear that is a pleasure to hold. Both she and her brother Sidney have a trusting look that will melt your heart. Mr. Goodbar is a full three feet tall and has claws that make him look like a real bear. Like many of Joan's bears, he has mink eyelashes that give him a special wide-eyed look. Baby-faced Clarissa also has elegant eyelashes.

Clarissa is 12 inches tall and jointed; she is made of German mohair and wears a lace collar and a bow.

Mr. Goodbar is 36 inches tall and jointed; he is made of German synthetic fur, wears a top hat, glasses, a collar and tie, and a vest that's decorated with political memorabilia.

Pamela Wooley

Pamela Wooley is a perfectionist. She makes teddy bears with great skill and attention to detail, so that each one is as charming as he or she can be. Pamela uses the best materials she can find, including European mohair, llama, and wool fur. Before she considers a bear to be finished, Pamela carefully trims the teddy bear from top to bottom; the result is a teddy bear that appears to be practically seamless. She doesn't want her bear's expression to be buried in messy, untrimmed fur. Pamela does all the work of making Wooley Bear Cottage bears herself, and she makes about 200 teddies each year—all of them as perfect as Pamela can make them.

Pamela's bears Kelsey and Katie wear nothing more than black bow ties; they don't need costumes to define their distinctive characters. He is a determined little bear that will always cheer you up when you're feeling down. She is a caring teddy bear, not the least bit vain or frivolous.

Laura is a glamorous teddy bear. Her costume is a fairly simple lace collar decorated with ribbons and flowers, but Laura's wavy mohair fur glistens to perfection. She would never think of going to bed before giving her fur the requisite 100 strokes with a soft hairbrush. Laura's bright eyes sparkle with excitement; she looks like she's just finished dressing for a party and is waiting for her escort to arrive.

Kelsey and *Katie* are 12 inches tall and jointed; they are made of mohair and wear bows.

Laura is 14 inches tall and jointed; she is made of German wavy mohair and wears an antique-lace collar.

Nona Woolley

Nona Woolley sews each teddy bear that she makes by hand. She enjoys watching a bear come to life in her hands. Nona likes to think about what each bear will mean to the person who takes it home. While she doesn't want to name her bears and give them specific identities—she leaves that up to you—Nona designs her bears to convey a special message to everyone who picks them up. Nona's bear Fool for Love is simultaneously happy and sad, shy and forthcoming; he looks as though he is madly in love and doesn't care who knows it.

Nona's bear Father Christmas is not the cheery Santa Claus that you see in store windows; he seems ancient and has a serious look on his face. The little figure in his long red robe is followed by a goat that carries the gifts Father Christmas will deliver. Nona says that she wants this bear to remind people to give of themselves without wanting anything in return.

While Nona will say that her favorite bear is the one she is currently working on, she is very fond of a bear she once made for a little boy. The boy's older brother had been given a very special teddy bear that had belonged to his father while he was growing up. The younger son also wanted a bear, so his mother asked Nona to copy the old bear. Now Old Ted and New Ted live happily with the two brothers.

Fool for Love is 15 inches tall and jointed; he is made of German mohair dyed to make his costume, wears a felt hat, and holds a bauble.

Father Christmas is 12 inches tall and jointed; he is made of mohair plush and wears a velvet coat with real-fur trim, a wool hat, and a leather belt with a silver buckle. His goat is made of wool and carries two baskets stuffed with miniature toys.

Beverly Martin Wright _____

When Beverly Martin Wright was three years old, her little brown teddy bear was taken away from her and given to a crying baby who was disturbing a party. Her bear was never returned, and Beverly still misses the little friend that once shared her secret world. Even though she has made more than 2,400 teddies, Beverly has never been able to replace her lost teddy bear.

Beverly started sewing when she was a young girl. While she was growing up, the sewing machine was always set up on the kitchen table. With two daughters to make clothes for, Beverly's mother was nearly always sewing. By watching her mom, Beverly picked up the skills that she now uses for bear making.

Teddy bears have a special relationship with their human friends. Beverly doesn't want to impose herself on this very personal association, so she doesn't give names or identities to the bears she makes. She leaves that to the person who will take the bear home. While she is creating a bear, Beverly tries to imagine a teddy that communicates empathy, love, and tranquility. She hopes that the good thoughts she tries to impart to her bears can be seen in the little faces of her teddies. Beverly calls her teddy bears the Wright Bears, and they come in many sizes and colors. Beverly hopes that children as well as grown-ups will fall in love with her bears, so she makes them with safety eyes, which can't break.

These jointed bears are 11 inches tall.

The **Wright Bears** are made of German mohair and come with ribbon bows. This Wright Bear is 15 inches tall and fully jointed.

These bears are 11 and 15 inches tall.

*This **Wright Bear** is 11 inches tall.*

Manufactured Teddy Bears

Almost everybody wants at least one teddy bear to hug, and teddy-bear manufacturers are hard at work making lovable bears and getting them into shops, where you can buy them and take them home. Teddy bears have an almost universal appeal. Some toys are designed for boys, others for girls, and a few toys, mostly games, are intended for both. When teddy bears were first introduced, manufacturers expected them to be bought for boys. But right away girls wanted to play with teddy bears too. Today about 60 percent of plush toys, including teddy bears, are bought for girls, indicating that teddy-bear manufacturers have continued to design and manufacture a toy that both boys and girls want to play with.

Christmas is the biggest season for giving teddy bears, but many people think that they also make terrific birthday gifts, especially for newborns. Nearly half of all the teddy bears that are sold in the United States are not gifts; people buy the bears for themselves. We buy most of our teddy bears in specialty shops, not large toy or department stores, which explains the success of the teddy-bear manufacturers you'll meet in the following pages.

For the most part, these manufacturers specialize in teddy bears; they primarily make high-quality bears and sell them to small shops rather than large-scale distributors.

The technology of teddy-bear manufacturing has advanced along with other technologies, but some commercial bearmakers still make teddies partially by hand. Other manufacturers use technology to make bears that look as though they were handmade. Some companies make traditional teddies using synthetic fur the colors of real bear fur; others make brightly colored bears that don't look anything like bears in nature. Some manufactured teddies are jointed and have movable heads, shoulders, and knees. Other bears aren't jointed so that they're very cuddly, while still others have flexible armatures that let them hold any pose. Manufactured teddies come in all shapes and sizes. Teddy bears are produced in factories all over the world by some companies that have made bears for more than 80 years and by other companies that began making teddies only recently. But no matter what color their plush is or what country they were manufactured in, all teddy bears are ambassadors of love.

Platinum Edition Snuffles by **Gund.**

Applause

Applause is a privately owned company with annual sales exceeding $100 million. The company specializes in high-quality stuffed toys, including teddy bears, and sells exclusively to gift shops, boutiques, and toy shops. Applause holds licenses for Smurfs, Sesame Street, characters created by Steven Spielberg, and many Walt Disney characters. A second division of the company produces plush toys that are associated with companies and organizations, such as Sony, Shell (Canada), Anheuser-Busch, Hardee's, and the Girl Scouts of America.

Like several other major toy manufacturers, Applause has turned to independent bearmakers for new product ideas. The company has licensed the designs of Robert Raikes, a successful bearmaker. Not long after he began making bears, Raikes found that the demand for his bears far exceeded his ability to turn out one-of-a-kind teddy bears. But the unique quality of his designs made it nearly impossible for Robert to establish a cottage industry on his own. His bears have hand-carved wooden faces, and to mass produce them, Raikes would have had to find skilled wood carvers who could duplicate his style of carving. Applause had the technical knowledge and trained workers that were needed to manufacture large numbers of Raikes's bears.

The Applause Raikes Bears are beautiful, faithful reproductions of Raikes's original teddy bears. Robert Raikes works closely with the company to develop and produce new designs. He also attends teddy-bear shows and conventions all over the United States, where he signs Applause bears for their adoring owners. The company's attention to detail in the manufacture of Raikes bears and all their products has made Applause one of the most successful American toy manufacturers.

Kiwi Koala is available in two sizes: 12 and 7 inches; he is jointed and made of plush.

Tyrone (left) and *Maude* (right) are Raikes Bears. He is 36 inches tall; she is 24 inches tall. They are jointed, made of plush, and have wooden faces and paws. He wears a velvet tux with satin trim. She wears a satin dress and hat, and a long strand of fake pearls.

MacIntosh is made in four sizes: 9, 12, 18, and 24 inches; he is unjointed and made of plush.

Rembrandt is available in two sizes: 10 and 12 inches. He is made of plush.

The **René Bears** in the bassinet are 16 inches tall; the larger bears are 24 inches tall. They're all unjointed and made of plush.

Catherine is part of the Remembrance Collection. She is 17½ inches tall and unjointed. Catherine is made of plush and wears a cotton dress with lace trim.

P.J. Bear is available in two sizes: 13 and 9½ inches; he is unjointed and made of plush.

Roosevelt is made in two sizes 11 and 13 inches; he is unjointed and made of plush.

Boz Bear is 12 inches tall and unjointed; he is made of plush.

Bearly There

Linda Spiegel, founder of Bearly There, was one of the first teddy-bear artists to start her own cottage industry. As soon as Linda started making bears, the demand for her teddies exceeded her ability to produce them. She hired helpers and set up a small factory. Building on Linda's initial success, Bearly There grew and expanded. The company now has more than 20 full-time workers, including Linda, who designs bears, makes patterns, purchases materials, and directs sales. The staff of Bearly There is made up primarily of women, many of whom used to be unemployed, unskilled workers living on welfare. Making teddy bears enables these women to support themselves and their families.

Linda spends part of every year traveling to teddy-bear shows, visiting the shops that sell her bears, and swapping stories about teddy bears with everyone she meets. She also conducts workshops for beginning bearmakers. Each season Linda introduces a new line of teddy-bear characters. From Silly Basil in the 1970s to Gus in the 1980s, her bears have a distinctive look that makes them instantly identifiable as Bearly There bears.

Treasure Ted *is about 15 inches tall, and he's made of distressed mohair.*

Gus *is 12 inches tall and made of acrylic fur.*

Berg Spielwaren

Bromo is 30 inches long and unjointed. He is made of vinyl fiber.

At the end of World War II, the Berg brothers returned to civilian life with nothing more than their uniforms and army blankets. In order to make a living, they decided to make stuffed toys. The Bergs cut up their uniforms and blankets, and transformed them into little toy animals, using their uniform buttons for the animals' eyes. The Bergs traded the toys for K rations and American cigarettes, which they swapped for more uniforms and blankets. They set up a jury-rigged production line in a farmhouse in Fieberbrunn. The little animals quickly became so popular that the Bergs often had difficulty obtaining enough materials to keep up with demand.

By 1951 the Berg brothers could afford to buy woven plush. The first animals they made from this luxurious fabric were teddy bears. They also made monkeys, rabbits, tigers, and foxes, replacing the uniform-button eyes with lifelike glass eyes. Their toys were exhibited in Vienna and at trade fairs in England, France, Italy, and Switzerland. Eventually Berg stuffed toys were shown at the Nuremberg Toy Fair, where buyers from all over the world come to see the best-made toys that are available, and Berg Spielwaren gained an international reputation for excellence.

The Bergs call their toys "animals with a heart" because each one has a bright red heart attached to its chest. Their line of stuffed animals includes many species, but the steadfast little teddy bear remains a favorite. Each year Berg makes teddies in several colors and sizes.

Ceri is 22 inches tall and unjointed. He is made of vinyl fiber.

R. Dakin & Company

Richard Dakin started his San Francisco company in 1955. He initially planned to import handmade shotguns and other sporting goods from Spain and Italy. When his son Roger joined the firm in 1957, Dakin expanded the product line to include bicycles, sailboats, woodenware, and toys. The first toy that Dakin imported was a battery-operated replica of the Zephyr, a historic train operated by the Southern Pacific Railroad. When the sample toy train arrived, it was packed with six small, velveteen animals. The stuffed toys seemed a lot more exciting than the locomotive, so Roger Dakin showed them to a buyer for a local department store. He immediately got an order for 300 stuffed animals. Dakin called the little animals Dream Pets, and they changed the direction of the company from importing to the manufacture of plush toys.

Two important decisions were made at the outset of Dakin's new business venture: All designs were to be created in house by a staff of designers, and Dakin toys were to be priced to sell as impulse purchases. Plush toys immediately proved to be the right direction for the Dakin company. Harold Nizamian, who took over the business in 1966, has expanded on the Dakin family's initial success. The company still manufactures relatively inexpensive stuffed toys, but it now also has a more-expensive line, Elégante.

Garfield in all his many variations is one of Dakin's best-loved toys. This born-to-party tomcat even has his own teddy bear named Pookie. Dakin also makes other teddies, including the best-selling Cuddles. This bear comes in several sizes and lifts his arms out to you in a way that seems to say, "Love me. Take me home."

Cuddles Bears are 14 inches tall and unjointed.

Shong Shong Panda is 27½ inches tall and unjointed. A 16-inch version of this bear is also available.

Big Cuddles Bears are 18 inches tall and unjointed.

Bride and *Groom Bears* are 7 inches tall; she wears a bridal gown, and he has on a morning suit.

From left to right: **Nancy Bear Nurse, Dr. Teddy, M.D.,** and **Karate Bear.** *These unjointed, plush bears are 7 inches tall. Their cotton uniforms are removable.*

Johann Hermann began making toy bears in 1907 in the German town of Sonneberg, which was a toy-making center. The American export house of George Borgfeldt & Company, which brought the first Steiff bears to the United States, was located in Sonneberg, as were many other important exporters, including S.S. Kresge and F.W. Woolworth.

Johann Hermann's children worked in his factory, and his son Bernhard founded his own toy company. This business flourished, and Bernhard's sons, Werner and Artur, came to work in his factory when they grew up. They had studied design, sculpture, and pattern making, and brought these skills to the family business.

After World War II, Sonneberg was in the Soviet-occupied zone, and in 1951 the Hermann family decided to move their factory to Hirschaid in the American zone. The company became known as Gebrüder Hermann KG. It's still a family business: Werner is the product manager in charge of design and quality control, and Artur handles sales and the financial aspects of the business. Their daughters are also active in the company and recently traveled to the United States to meet teddy-bear collectors.

Hermann has made teddy bears for more than 80 years, but the company also makes stuffed horses, donkeys, and elephants mounted on wheels. All Hermann animals, even their frogs, have a special cuddly roundness. Hermann stuffed bears are easily identified by their red pressed-plastic logos, with the word "Teddy" in gold-colored script across the center of the disk.

Bear Lying is 26 inches long and unjointed; he is made of mink plush. This bear is available in three additional sizes: 12, 16, and 20 inches.

Bernhard Bear is 22 inches tall and wears a vest and a bow tie.

Nostalgic Teddy Bears are jointed and made of mohair; they range in size from 3 to 24 inches.

Gebrüder Hermann

Teddy School includes a teacher bear, which is 14 inches tall and wears a tie, and six student bears, which are 8 inches tall, wear children's clothes, and carry school bags. The set comes with six benches, six student's desks, a teacher's desk, and a blackboard.

Nostalgic Teddy Bear is jointed and made of mohair; he is made in a range of sizes from 3 to 24 inches.

Gund

Baron is made in two sizes: 28 inches and 24 inches. He is made of multifilament plush and has a shaved muzzle and a leather nose.

Adolph Gund immigrated to the United States in 1898. He planned to found a company that would produce high-quality stuffed toys, and he did. Gund is one of the largest and most successful toymakers in the world. Gund has also been making teddy bears longer than any other American company. Gund introduced its first teddy bear in 1906. When William Taft became President, Gund produced Billy Possum, but it never enjoyed the same popularity as Roosevelt's bear.

Gund's first headquarters were in Connecticut, but the company soon moved into New York City, where a 14-year-old boy named Jacob Swedlin came to work for the firm as a janitor. He was eager to learn the toy business, and Adolph Gund, who had no children, began to teach Swedlin about making plush toys. Jacob Swedlin took over management of the company in the 1920s when Adolph Gund retired, but he promised to retain the Gund family name. Jacob's three brothers also joined the firm, and his daughter Rita's husband, Herbert Raiffe, became president of the family business in 1969. Rita Raiffe is head of design, and under her leadership Gund has become one of the leading manufacturers of soft, huggable plush toys.

Gund produced toys under a license from Walt Disney in the 1950s, and the company now makes Bialosky Bears. Following the success of their book, *The Teddy Bear Catalog,* Peggy and Alan Bialosky worked with Gund designers to produce a version of their old bear. While Gund's Bialosky doesn't look very much like Peggy and Alan's original teddy, which is a Steiff bear, he has a very special charm of his own and the same feeling as the older bear.

Snuffles is probably Gund's best-loved bear. He is soft, lovable, and beautifully made, like all Gund teddy bears. Snuffles comes in many sizes and colors. Gund also makes softer-than-soft baby animals for babies, and a series of collectible bears for grown-ups.

Gear Bear is 23 inches tall. He is unjointed and wears overalls. A 9½-inch and 16-inch bear are also available.

Kiwi is 11 inches tall and unjointed. A 15-inch koala is also available.

Tinker is available in two sizes: 25 inches and 19 inches. The bear is jointed and has a velvet ribbon.

Creampuff is made in two sizes: 16 inches and 19 inches. The bear is unjointed.

Commemorative Bear (left) is 16 inches tall and jointed; he wears a ribbon and has a permanently attached leather badge of authority. **Gundy** (right) is 9 inches tall and comes with a ribbon tie and an American flag.

House of Nisbet

Peggy Nisbet created a portrait doll of Queen Elizabeth II in honor of her coronation in 1953. This beautiful doll was the beginning of a new business. Peggy's daughter Alison Wilson and her husband, Jack Wilson, are active in the company, which has been called the House of Nisbet since 1975.

Jack decided that the firm ought to make teddy bears as well as dolls after he read Peter Bull's *The Teddy Bear Book.* Jack Wilson and Peter Bull worked together to create Bully Bear. The stuffed bear comes in a variety of sizes and is the subject of several books. In 1983 Nisbet republished Peter Bull's book, which had been out of print for many years. That same year Wilson and Bull also began working on the Zodiac Bears with illustrator Pauline MacMillian. Each bear in this series of 12 has the characteristics of a person born under the sign of the zodiac that the bear represents.

Jack has also created a bear that evokes memories of childhood. Jack's Bear has the look and feel of an old bear because he's made of cuddly, distressed alpaca. At the 1987 toy fair, Nisbet introduced a new kind of teddies, Body Language Bears. These plush bears can assume hundreds of different poses. Instead of being jointed in the traditional way, this innovative bear has a bendable armature that allows him to hold any pose you put him in. Nisbet also makes the Celebrity Collection. These ten bears and one rabbit are closely associated with leading children's writers or well-known bearmakers, including Carol-Lynn Rössel Waugh, Linda Mullins, and Howard R. Gares (creator of the Uncle Wiggly stories).

Mr. Do-It Bear is 13 inches tall; he is a replica of one of the antique bears collected by Linda Mullins.

Body Language Bear is 15 inches tall and has a flexible skeleton. He is made of mohair and wears a scarf. A special component in each foot connects the bear to an included stand.

Delicatessen Replica *is made in two sizes: 25 inches and 15 inches. The fully jointed bears are made of distressed mohair and come with scarves and flight bags.*

Body Language Bear *is made of plush and can hold any pose.*

Delicatessen in Hollywood *is 18 inches tall and jointed; he is made of distressed mohair and wears a T-shirt and scarf.*

361

Merrythought

Guardsman (left), *London Policeman* (top), and *Beefeater* (right) are 18 inches tall and made of mohair.

Merrythought did not begin making teddy bears until 1930. When the company's founders, W.G. Holmes and G.H. Laxton, became partners in 1919, they planned to operate a spinning mill in Yorkshire, England. They never expected to become "toymakers to the King." Their mill produced mohair yarn, which was much in demand until the invention of synthetic fibers in the 1920s. That's when Holmes and Laxton decided to make stuffed toys. In order to save their business, the partners purchased a plush-fabric weaving factory and hired a production manager and a sales manager who had experience in the toy business. Holmes, Laxton, and Co. leased space from the Coalbrookdale Iron Company and began manufacturing Merrythought plush toys.

During World War II, the factory was converted to war work, but toy production resumed in 1946. Trayton Holmes took charge of the firm in 1949, and under his guidance Merrythought modernized and expanded its operations. To increase production Merrythought imported an automatic stuffing machine from the United States. As the company grew, more space was rented from Coalbrookdale, and in 1956 Merrythought bought the iron company's 1889 brick factory building on the Severn River in Shropshire, which is now the company's main manufacturing facility.

Merrythought has made stuffed versions of American cartoon characters, including the famous MGM cat-and-mouse team, Tom and Jerry. One of the most-popular Merrythought bears is named Cheeky. He was first introduced in 1955, and he's still in production. Like all Merrythought toys, Cheeky is a good-quality teddy bear with a good, warm feeling.

Highlander is 36 inches tall and made of mohair. He comes fully costumed.

North American Bear Co.

Barbara Isenberg, founder of North American Bear Co., created her first bear in 1978. Albert the Running Bear was a present for her son, Christopher. Barbara couldn't draw and she couldn't sew, but she had the vision and determination to actualize her ideas about teddy bears. Even though Barbara's first bear was made for a child, she knew that she wanted to create teddy bears for grown-ups. Barbara felt that adults would respond to the special whimsy of her V.I.B.s (Very Important Bears), so she made the bears large (20 inches), cuddly, and colorful, and gave them very funny names. The first four V.I.B.s were Chef Bearnaise, Scarlett O'Beara, Douglas Bearbanks, and Amelia Bearhart.

The first North American Bear Co. teddies were manufactured in the United States in an out-of-date factory. When Barbara's brother joined the business, he helped Barbara move production to Asia, where most soft toys are now manufactured and where the latest technology, best materials, and most-skilled workers are readily available. The firm's designers and sample makers still work in the United States, and in 1987 they moved from the basement of a house in Greenwich Village to a loft near the New York Toy Center.

North American now makes bunnies and other animals as well as the VanderBears, an elegantly dressed family of well-to-do teddy bears. One measure of the company's success is the high prices that collectors are willing to pay for V.I.B.s that are no longer in production. Amelia Bearhart, for example, is currently valued at over $1,000.

Lula and *Be-Bop* are 9 inches tall, unjointed, and made of plush. She wears a felt skirt, a polo shirt, and saddle shoes; he wears pants, a shirt and tie, and saddle shoes.

Humphrey Beargart and *Lauren Bearcall* are 20 inches tall and unjointed. He wears wool pants, a trench coat, and a felt hat. She wears a fake-fur coat and net hat.

The **VanderBear Family** from left to right: **Cornelius** (20 inches), **Fluffy** (12 inches), **Alice** (18 inches), **Muffy** (7 inches), and **Fuzzy** (12 inches). These fully jointed bears are made of plush. Their "A Day in the Country" outfits are made of denim, cotton print, and chambray, and include straw hats.

James Beard is 20 inches tall and wears pants, a cotton cook's jacket with kerchief, and a chef's hat.

Cub Canabearal is 20 inches tall and unjointed; he is made of brown plush and dressed in a flight suit.

ARRIVALS

REMBEARANDT
ABNY
BUDDY
PANDAS
BAGELS

CHARLES LINDBEARGH
BEBOP & LULA
LARGE WRAGGLES
BLACK NIBBLES
CHILD BEARER

DEPARTURES

STATUE OF LIBEARTY
NAPOLEON BEARNAPARTE
DOUGLAS BEARBANKS
QUEEN ELIZABEAR

FARM
AUNT
IGGY
TIPPE

TRACK 1

TRA

The New York Times

During rush hour in the train station, you'll encounter **Albert the Running Bear** and **Violet the Exercise Bear** (20-inch bears dressed in sweats), **Baby's Bears** (soft, white bears, 10 and 14 inches tall), **Pandas** (10, 15, and 20 inches tall), **HUG** (19 inches) and **Buddy** (13 inches) in Bear Aid T-shirts, **Bagels** (10 inches), **ABNY** and **L'IL ABNY** (13 and 8 inches tall, wearing sweaters with mortarboard logos), **Mr. Beeps** (13 inches tall with a black noisy nose), **Be-Bop** and **Lula** (dancing bears from the 1950s), **Childbearer** (a 9-inch plush stork carrying a baby bear), **Harvey** (a 15-inch white rabbit), **Jack the Party Animal, Wraggles** (plush puppies), and **Nibbles** (black rabbits).

North American Bear Co. ——————

Bearilyn Monroe *is 20 inches tall and wears a sun dress, a scarf, lace panties, and sunglasses.*

Russ Berrie and Company

Russ Berrie began his company in his garage in Palisades Park, New Jersey, in 1964. His first product was a disgustingly irresistible creature that looked a little like Humpty Dumpty, but more than 10 million people decided to buy Bupkis. Since that time the company's product line has increased to about 4,000 different items, including plush toys, greeting cards, statuettes, key chains, ceramic mugs, and T-shirts. Russ Berrie and Company products are sold in more than 70,000 gift shops in airports, hotels, and hospitals.

Unlike many other toy or gift companies, Russ Berrie and Company does not manufacture any of its own products. The firm uses factories around the world to produce the plush toys and other items it designs and sells. By doing this, the company is able to create items from the best and most-appropriate materials, and to use whatever technology is needed; production is not restricted by the limitations of a company-owned factory. Each of the firm's products is made in a facility that is particularly suited to manufacturing it.

One of the company's most-endearing stuffed toys is the teddy bear Snuggle. This spokes-bear has delighted everyone who's seen a Snuggle commercial on television. The teddy bounces around on piles of sheets and towels, advertising Snuggle Fabric Softener. Snuggle is a basic teddy bear—cute as can be and ready to reach out to you with love and hugs.

Russ Berrie feels that success comes from doing what you do best and making the most of your own particular talents. The enormous success of his company bears this out. Russ Berrie and Company is a world leader in the gift industry. The firm is continuously developing new ideas, efficiently bringing them into production, and effectively getting them into shops, where most of us will find them irresistible.

© Russ Berrie and Company, Inc.

Boudoir Bear is 10 inches tall and wears a lace teddy.

Born to . . . Bears are 6 inches tall and made of nonallergenic, synthetic materials.

Steiff

Margarete Steiff was a dressmaker in the small German town of Giengen. She began making stuffed toys for her nieces in 1880 and gradually developed a small toy-making business. Richard Steiff, Margarete's nephew, joined the company in 1897, and the family-owned business began to expand rapidly. Steiff started making teddy bears in 1903. These jointed bears were based on Richard's design and were considered to be very unusual at the time. But Steiff bears sold so well in the United States that by 1907 the company was producing a million bears a year.

The firm built a new factory to meet the increased production demands. The large glass and metal structure offered excellent working conditions with plenty of bright light and panoramic views of the wooded countryside nearby. Margarete Steiff, the founder of the company, oversaw production until her death in 1909, and Steiff has remained a family business. This large company still resembles a cottage industry in many ways. Most people who live in Giengen work for Steiff. This "company town," with its cobblestone streets and story-book houses, is the perfect setting for a teddy-bear factory.

Since 1904 Steiff has identified its teddy bears and stuffed animals with a metal button in the ear. The company has always produced many kinds of animals, as well as gnomes and elves, but Steiff bears are the company's mainstay. Old bears are treasured and scarce, so Steiff has begun reissuing their early bears. These beautifully crafted new bears make venerable Steiff bears accessible to collectors and other people who want a good bear to hug.

Teddy Bear Replica 1909 in four sizes: 9¾, 11, 20, and 23½ inches. The bears are jointed and made of mohair.

Dicky Bear is 12½ inches tall and fully jointed. He is made of mohair and has painted paw pads.

Original Teddy Bears *in five sizes:*
29¼, 19, 16, 14, and 10 inches. The
smallest bear is wired; the others are
fully jointed. All the teddies are made
of mohair and have shoe-button eyes.

Circus Dolly Bears (three shown) are reproductions of bears originally made in 1913. They are 12 inches tall, jointed, and made of mohair.

Margaret Strong Bride and *Groom Bears* are 14 inches tall, fully jointed, and made of mohair. The bride wears a cotton-lace gown and a veil; the groom wears wool pants and jacket, and a top hat.

Trudy

Benjamin Bear in four sizes: 8, 11, 15, and 28 inches. These bears wear T-shirts imprinted with a company logo.

Like many other European and American toy companies, Trudy began as a small toymaker and grew into a much larger company. But toward the end of the 1970s, the business began to falter; sales were down and expenses were up. The company was offered for sale, and Peter Burnham and his brother Bill decided to buy it. Even though they had not been planning to get into the stuffed-toy industry, Trudy seemed like the right company for them. They were looking for a manufacturing firm that they could build together and at the same time stay close to home. The Burnham brothers purchased Trudy in 1979. Peter handles the financial aspects of the business and domestic manufacturing, while Bill handles marketing and overseas production.

Trudy produces its own plush-toy designs as well as making premiums for other companies, including Crave Cat Food, Almaden Vineyards, Starkist Tuna, and Nestlé. Trudy also makes Sleepy Time Bear, which is named for Celestial Seasonings' popular tea, and Spuds MacKenzie, the spokesdog for Bud Light beer.

While many toymakers manufacture their products in Europe or Asia, Trudy produces many of its stuffed toys in the United States. The firm has a new factory in Norwalk, Connecticut, that employs nearly 100 workers. The facility is in an area that has a very high unemployment rate, and Trudy is participating in a government-sponsored program to encourage industry to expand into economically distressed areas. The Burnham brothers count the good will that their factory has generated in Norwalk as one of their major assets.

Reggie (four shown) is 15 inches tall and comes with an alphabet T-shirt and coloring book.

Acknowledgments

Joanne Adams, 137 Cottonwood Trail, Silver Creek, Park City, UT 84060

Durae Allen, 7094 Ridge Rd., Hanover, MD 21076

Darci & Scott Andrews, 200 Franz Valley School Rd., Calistoga, CA 94515

Applause Inc., 6101 Variel, Woodland Hills, CA 91367

Celia Baham, 1562 San Joaquin Ave., San Jose, CA 95118

Reneé Koch Bane, 4294 Sierra Ave., Norco, CA 91760

Jody Battaglia, 1603 Exeter Ct., Marietta, GA 30068

Bearly There, Inc., 14782 Moran St., West Westminster, CA 92683

Doris Beck, 15913 S.E. 8th St., Bellevue, WA 98008

Berg Spielwaren, Rosenegg 66, A-6391 Fieberbrunn, Austria

Catherine Bordi, Route 1, Box 10-C, Eastsound, WA 98245

Loretta Botta, 1231-42nd Ave., San Francisco, CA 94122

Mary Ellen Brandt, 825 7th St. S.E., Oelwein, IA 50662

Deanna Brittsan, 1155 Uppingham, Thousand Oaks, CA 91360

Genie Buttitta, 942 Brighton Rd., Tonawanda, NY 14150

Pam Carlson, 2961 S.W. Turner Rd., West Linn, OR 97068

Pat Carriker

Lynda Carswell, 115 Gennessee, San Francisco, CA 94112

Deri Cartier, P.O. Box 1110, Washougal, WA 98671

Carol Cavallaro, 162 Nortontown Rd., Madison, CT 06443

Barbara Conley & Tracey Roe, 792 S. 3rd St., San Jose, CA 95112

Cindy Coombs, 1827 Louise Rd., Lugoff, SC 29078

Candy Corvari, 19005 4th Ave. S.W., Seattle, WA 98166

Anne E. Cranshaw, 8 Stark Rd., Worcester, MA 01602

Nancy Crowe, 2400 Woodview Dr., Lansing, MI 48911

R. Dakin & Company, Inc., Box 7746, San Francisco, CA 94120

Suzanne De Pee, 2208 S. Valley Dr., Visalia, CA 93277

Brenda Dewey, Box 863, Clinton, NY 13323

Denise Dewire, 27 W. Prospect St., Ventura, CA 93001

Sylvia Dombrowski, 200 Rhoads Ave., Haddonfield, NJ 08033

Tatum Egelin, 1447 Wallace Ave., Los Angeles, CA 90026

Martha Fain, 8015 Montero Dr., Prospect, KY 40059

Barbara Ferrier, 441 Sacramento, Nevada City, CA 95959

Patricia Fici, 418 Revere Dr., Monroeville, PA 15146

Sandy Fleming, 52-695 Avenida Ramirez, La Quinta, CA 92253

Etta Foran & Pat Joho, 409 S. May, Joliet, IL 60436

Joyce Francies, 1106 Debbie Ln., Placerville, CA 95667

Gloria & Mike Franks, Goose Creek Farm, Pullman, WV 26421

Diane Gard, 1005 W. Oak St., Fort Collins, CO 80521

Lori Gardiner, 2565 S. Mayflower, Arcadia, CA 91006

Gebrüder Hermann KG, Amlingstadter Str 9, D-8606 Hirschaid, West Germany

Dolores & LeRoy Gould, 6453 N. Fairfield, Chicago, IL 60645

Nancy Green, 606 Berkshire Dr., Garner, NC 27529

Dolores Groseck, 443 Militia Hill, Southampton, PA 18966

Gund, Inc., One Runyons Ln., Edison, NJ 08817

Hope Hatch, P.O. Box 397, North San Juan, CA 95960

Frances Hayden, P.O. Box 250, Damariscotta, ME 04543

Billee Henderson, 9312 Santayana Dr., Fairfax, VA 22031

Miriam Hertz, 15410 N.W. Melody Ct., Beaverton, OR 97006

Dee Hockenberry, 14191 Bacon Rd., Albion, NY 14411

Donna Hodges, 7855 Avenida Navidad, San Diego, CA 92122

Mary Holstad, 17831-145th Ave. S.E., Renton, WA 98058

House of Nisbet, Ltd., 18A Ashombe Park Road, Weston Super Mare, Avon BS23 2YE, England

Nancy Howlan & Virginia Jasmer, 1962 Lomond Ave., Springfield, OR 97477

Hillary Hulen & David Reugg, 7804 Wagner Creek Rd., Talent, OR 97540

Ann Inman, 11602 Norton Ave., Chino, CA 91710

Trudy Jacobson, 7801 N. Wade School, Columbia, MO 65202

Jerry & Morgan Jurdan, Route 1, Box 467, Amboy, WA 98601

Charlotte Kane, 56 Blodgett Ave., Swampscott, MA 01907

Doris King, 4353 Landolt Ave., Sacramento, CA 95821

Sue Kruse, 431 Wooden Dr., Placentia, CA 92670

Jacque Kudner, 1727 Maybrook Rd., Jackson, MI 49203

Sharon Lapointe, 1782 Tracy Ln., Auburn, CA 95603

Mary Kaye Lee, 2460 W. Quinn Ave., Littleton, CO 80120

Althea Leistikow, 1025 S.W. Taylor, Topeka, KS 66612

Lynn Lumley, 1600 Airport Rd., Carson City, NV 89701

Jeanie Major, 3277 Long Lake Rd. S.E., Port Orchard, WA 98366

Chuck & Judy Malinski, 1019 S. Chantilly, Anaheim, CA 92806

Cleo Marshall, 457 Sierra Point Rd., Brisbane, CA 94005

Carol Martin, 515 N. Fourth St., Arkansas City, KS 67005

Bonnie Waas McCabe, 81 Pleasant St., Hoffman Estates, IL 60194

Maureen McElwain, 3209 Marie Dr., Raleigh, NC 27604

Flora Mediate, 190 Malcolm Dr., Pasadena, CA 91105

Ted Menten, 300 E. 40 St., New York, NY 10016

Doris & Terry Michaud, 505 W. Broad St., Chesaning, MI 48616

Joanne Mitchell, 3502 Rolling Terr., Spring, TX 77388

Kathy Mullin, 8840 Bold Ruler Way, Fair Oaks, CA 95628

Belinda & John Nesler, 423 Western, Findlay, OH 45840

Gary & Margaret Nett, 601 Taneytown Rd., Gettysburg, PA 17325

Sue Newlin, 519 S. Fifth Ave., Arcadia, CA 91006

Kaylee Nilan, 435 Main St., Etna, CA 96027

North American Bear Co., Inc., 401 N. Wabash, Chicago, IL 60611

Kathy Olsen, 8625 Westbrook Dr., Sturtevant, WI 53177

Mary Olsen, P.O. Box 264, Graham, WA 98338

Donna Focardi Pedini, Box 76, Killawog, NY 13794

Rose Policky, 264 W. Exchange, Astoria, OR 69162

Beverly Port, P.O. Box 711, Retsil, WA 98378

Kimberlee Port, P.O. Box 85534, Seattle, WA 98145-1534

Cynthia Powell, 8820 Swiftsail, Indianapolis, IN 46256

Reeves International, Inc., 1107 Broadway, New York, NY 10010

Betsy Reum, 1303 Moores River Dr., Lansing, MI 48910

Saki Romerhaus, 951 S. Alvord Blvd., Evansville, IN 47714

Russ Berrie and Company, Inc., 111 Bauer Dr., Oakland, NJ 07436

Kathy & Owen Sandusky, 25629 Oak St., Lomita, CA 90717

Laurie Sasaki, 2221 Parker St., Berkeley, CA 94704

Steve Schutt

Denis Shaw, P.O. Drawer A, La Honda, CA 94020

Linda Suzanne Shum, 7891 Fiesta Ln., Cupertino, CA 95014

Marcia Sibol, 424 Arbour Dr., Newark, DE 19713

Fred Slayter, 3020 N. Federal, Ft. Lauderdale, FL 33306

Smithsonian Institution, Washington, D.C. 20560

Sally Stearns, Highway 97 and Main, Stotts City, MO 65756

Judith Swanson, R.R. 1, Box 88-E, Kirkland, IL 60146

Tide-Rider, Inc., 85 Corporate Dr., Hauppauge, NY 11788

Trudy Corporation, 165 Water St., Norwalk, CT 06856

Laura Walker, 115 Liberty Ln., Washington, IL 61571

Kathleen Wallace, Box 329, Rd. #1, Spring City, PA 19475

Carol-Lynn Rössel Waugh, 5 Morrill, Winthrop, ME 04364

Beverly White, 399 Echo Dell Rd., Downingtown, PA 19335

Barbara Wiltrout, 12719 Bryant St., Yucaipa, CA 92399

Joan & Mike Woessner, 1150 Fern St., Escondido, CA 92027

Pamela Wooley, 5021 Stringtown Rd., Evansville, IN 47711

Nona Woolley, P.O. Box 4552, Rolling Bay, WA 98061

Beverly Martin Wright, 890 Patrol Rd., Woodside, CA 94062

Special thanks to **Eunice Barbee, David Brown, Kim Marquardt, Florence Skweres. Sean St. Onge, Lucy Tooper,** and the staff of **Bears To Go,** San Francisco.